Demographics and Run Timing of Adult Lost River (*Deltistes luxatus*) and Shortnose (*Chasmistes brevirostris*) Suckers in Upper Klamath Lake, Oregon, 2009

By David A. Hewitt, Brian S. Hayes, Eric C. Janney, Alta C. Harris, Justin P. Koller, and Mark A. Johnson

Prepared in cooperation with the Bureau of Reclamation

Open-File Report 2011–1088

U.S. Department of the Interior
U.S. Geological Survey

U.S. Department of the Interior
KEN SALAZAR, Secretary

U.S. Geological Survey
Marcia K. McNutt, Director

U.S. Geological Survey, Reston, Virginia: 2011

For more information on the USGS—the Federal source for science about the Earth, its natural and living resources, natural hazards, and the environment, visit http://www.usgs.gov or call 1-888-ASK-USGS.

For an overview of USGS information products, including maps, imagery, and publications, visit http://www.usgs.gov/pubprod

To order this and other USGS information products, visit *http://store.usgs.gov*

Suggested citation:
Hewitt, D.A., Hayes, B.S., Janney, E.C., Harris, A.C., Koller, J.P., and Johnson, M.A., 2011, Demographics and run timing of adult Lost River (*Deltistes luxatus*) and shortnose (*Chasmistes brevirostris*) suckers in Upper Klamath Lake, Oregon, 2009: U.S. Geological Survey Open-File Report 2011-1088, 38 p.

Contents

Executive Summary.. 1

Introduction... 3

Methods... 4

    Sampling and Fish Handling 4

    Remote Passive Integrated Transponder Tag Detection Systems.. 5

    Survival Analysis 5

    Recruitment and Population Rate of Change... 7

    Size Composition Analysis 8

Results... 9

    Lost River Suckers 9

        Catch Summary and Run Timing for 2009 9

        Survival, Recruitment, and Size Composition...10

            Upper Klamath Lake Lakeshore Spawning Subpopulation 10

            Williamson and Sprague River Spawning Subpopulation 11

    Shortnose Suckers 13

        Catch Summary and Run Timing for 2009 13

        Survival, Recruitment, and Size Composition...14

Discussion 15

Acknowledgments 17

References Cited..18

Figures

Figure 1. Map showing sampling locations for Lost River suckers and shortnose suckers in
Upper Klamath Lake and its tributaries... 21

Figure 2. Seasonality of trammel net captures of Lost River suckers at lakeshore springs...................... 22

Figure 3. Seasonality of detections of Lost River suckers on remote passive integrated
transponder (PIT) tag antennas at lakeshore springs. 23

Figure 4. Seasonality of captures of Lost River suckers in the upstream trap of the Williamson River weir............... 24

Figure 5. Seasonality of detections of Lost River suckers on the remote passive integrated
transponder (PIT) tag antenna at the upstream trap of the Williamson River weir.............................. 25

Figure 6. Seasonality of detections of Lost River suckers on the remote passive integrated
transponder (PIT) tag antenna array across the Sprague River just downstream of the Chiloquin Dam site............... 26

Figure 7. Model-averaged estimates of apparent annual survival probability (Φ) and derived population
rate of change (λ) with 95% confidence intervals for Lost River suckers from the lakeshore spawning
subpopulation 27

Figure 8. Boxplots of fork lengths of male and female Lost River suckers captured in trammel nets at
lakeshore springs 28

Figure 9. Model-averaged estimates of apparent annual survival probability (Φ) with 95% confidence
intervals for Lost River suckers from the river spawning subpopulation 29

Figure 10. Boxplots of fork lengths of male and female Lost River suckers captured at pre-spawn
staging areas in Upper Klamath Lake and in the Williamson and Sprague Rivers 30

Figure 11. Seasonality of detections of shortnose suckers on the remote passive integrated
transponder (PIT) tag antenna at the upstream trap of the Williamson River weir.............................. 31

Figure 12. Model-averaged estimates of apparent annual survival probability (Φ) and derived population rate of change (λ) with 95% confidence intervals for shortnose suckers 32

Figure 13. Boxplots of fork lengths of male and female shortnose suckers captured in Upper Klamath Lake and the Williamson and Sprague Rivers 33

Tables

Table 1. Numbers of Lost River and shortnose suckers captured in Upper Klamath Lake (UKL) and the Williamson River 34

Table 2. Numbers of Lost River and shortnose suckers detected by remote antennas in Upper Klamath Lake (UKL) and its tributaries 35

Table 3. Model selection results for the top 10 capture-recapture models fitted to the data for the lakeshore spawning subpopulation of Lost River suckers. 36

Table 4. Model selection results for the top nine capture-recapture models fitted to the data for the river spawning subpopulation of Lost River suckers. 37

Table 5. Model selection results for the top six capture-recapture models fitted to the data for the shortnose sucker population 38

Conversion Factors and Acronyms

Conversion Factors

SI to Inch/Pound

Multiply	By	To obtain
Length		
centimeter (cm)	0.3937	inch (in.)
millimeter (mm)	0.03937	inch (in.)
meter (m)	3.281	foot (ft)
kilometer (km)	0.6214	mile (mi)
Flow rate		
cubic meter per second (m^3/s)	35.31	cubic foot per second (ft^3/s)

Temperature in degrees Celsius (°C) may be converted to degrees Fahrenheit (°F) as follows:

$$°F = (1.8 \times °C) + 32.$$

Acronyms

CJS	Cormack-Jolly-Seber
FDX	full-duplex
FL	fork length
LRS	Lost River sucker
PIT	passive integrated transponder
SNS	shortnose sucker
UKL	Upper Klamath Lake
USGS	U.S. Geological Survey

Demographics and Run Timing of Adult Lost River (*Deltistes luxatus*) and Shortnose (*Chasmistes brevirostris*) Suckers in Upper Klamath Lake, Oregon, 2009

By David A. Hewitt, Brian S. Hayes, Eric C. Janney, Alta C. Harris, Justin P. Koller, and Mark A. Johnson

Executive Summary

Data from a long-term capture-recapture program were used to assess the status and dynamics of populations of two long-lived, federally endangered catostomids in Upper Klamath Lake, Oregon. Lost River suckers (*Deltistes luxatus*) and shortnose suckers (*Chasmistes brevirostris*) have been captured and tagged with passive integrated transponder (PIT) tags during their spawning migrations in each year since 1995. In addition, beginning in 2005, individuals that had been previously PIT-tagged were re-encountered on remote underwater antennas deployed throughout the spawning areas. Captures and remote encounters during spring 2009 were used to describe the spawning migrations in that year and also were incorporated into capture-recapture analyses of population dynamics over the last decade. Cormack-Jolly-Seber (CJS) open population capture-recapture models were used to estimate annual survival probabilities, and a reverse-time analog of the CJS model was used to estimate recruitment of new individuals into the spawning populations. In addition, data on the size composition of captured fish was examined for any additional evidence of recruitment. Survival and recruitment estimates were combined to estimate changes in population size over time and to determine the status of the populations through 2007. Separate analyses were conducted for each species and also for each subpopulation of Lost River suckers (LRS). One subpopulation of LRS migrates into tributaries to spawn, similar to shortnose suckers (SNS), whereas the other subpopulation spawns at upwelling areas along the eastern shoreline of the lake.

In 2009, we captured and tagged 781 LRS at four shoreline areas and recaptured an additional 638 individuals that had been tagged in previous years. Across all four areas, the remote antennas detected 6,056 individual LRS during the spawning season. Spawning activity peaked in April and most individuals were encountered at Sucker Springs and Cinder Flats. In the Williamson River, we captured and tagged 3,008 LRS and 287 SNS, and recaptured 271 LRS and 81 SNS that had been tagged in previous years. Remote antennas that spanned the river downstream of the tributary spawning areas detected a total of 12,509 LRS and 5,023 SNS. Most LRS passed upstream in mid-April when water temperatures were rising and near or greater than 10 °C. In contrast, peaks in upstream passage of SNS occurred in late April and early May when water temperatures were rising and near or greater than 12 °C. Finally, an additional 1,569 LRS and 1,794 SNS were captured in trammel net sampling at pre-spawn staging areas in the northeastern portion of the lake. Of these, 209 of the LRS and 452 of the SNS had been PIT-tagged in previous years. For LRS, encounter histories showed that nearly all of the fish captured at the staging areas were members of the subpopulation that spawns in the tributaries.

Capture-recapture analyses for the LRS subpopulation that spawns at the shoreline areas included encounter histories for more than 9,000 individuals, and analyses for the subpopulation that spawns in the tributaries included more than 14,000 encounter histories. With a few exceptions, the survival of males and females in both subpopulations was high (> 0.9) between 1999 and 2007. Notably lower survival occurred for both sexes from the tributaries in 2000, for males from the shoreline areas in 2002, and for males from the tributaries in 2006. Recruitment of new individuals into either spawning population was trivial in all years between 2002 and 2007. Over that period, the abundance of males in the lakeshore spawning subpopulation declined by 44–53 percent and the abundance of females declined by 25–38 percent. Similarly, the abundance of males in the tributary spawning subpopulation declined by as much as 39 percent and the abundance of females declined by as much as 33 percent.

Capture-recapture analyses for SNS included encounter histories for more than 12,000 individuals. The majority of annual survival estimates between 2001 and 2007 were high (> 0.8), but SNS experienced more years of low survival than either LRS subpopulation. The survival of both sexes was particularly low in both 2001 and 2004, and male survival also was somewhat low in 2002 and 2006. Similar to LRS, recruitment of new individuals into the spawning population was trivial in all years between 2001 and 2007. Over that period, the abundance of male SNS declined by 58–80 percent and the abundance of females declined by 52–73 percent.

Despite relatively high survival in most years, both species have experienced substantial declines in the abundance of spawning fish because losses from mortality have not been balanced by recruitment of new individuals. Indeed, all populations appear to be largely comprised of fish that were present in the late 1990s and early 2000s. As a result, the status of the endangered sucker populations in Upper Klamath Lake remains worrisome, and the situation is most dire for shortnose suckers. Survival analyses show that the two species do not necessarily experience poor survival in the same years and that poor survival on an annual scale is not predictable from fish die-offs observed in the summer and fall. Future analyses will explore the connections between annual sucker survival and environmental factors of interest, such as water quality and disease. Our monitoring program provides a robust platform for estimating vital population parameters, evaluating the status of the populations, and assessing the effectiveness of conservation and recovery efforts.

Introduction

Lost River suckers (*Deltistes luxatus*) and shortnose suckers (*Chasmistes brevirostris*) are long-lived catostomids that are endemic to the Upper Klamath River basin in southern Oregon and northern California (Scoppettone and Vinyard, 1991). Historical accounts indicate that both species once were extremely abundant throughout the upper basin and were used in a subsistence fishery by Native Americans and later in a popular recreational snag fishery that was closed in 1987 (Markle and Cooperman, 2002). Declining population abundance trends and range reductions were noted for both species as early as the mid-1960s. The extent of these declines was not evident, however, until the mid-1980s, when recreational catch rates exhibited dramatic decreases that were attributable in part to overfishing (Markle and Cooperman, 2002; National Research Council, 2004). Estimated annual fishery harvest of spawning suckers in the Williamson and Sprague Rivers, tributaries to Upper Klamath Lake in Oregon, declined from more than 10,000 fish in 1968 to 687 fish in 1985 (Markle and Cooperman, 2002). In addition to declining catches, age data from suckers collected during a 1986 fish die-off indicated that the Lost River sucker (LRS) population was composed of old individuals and that no substantial recruitment had occurred during the previous 15 years (Scoppettone and Vinyard, 1991; U.S. Fish and Wildlife Service, 1993). These findings led to the federal listing of both species under the Endangered Species Act in 1988. Upper Klamath Lake probably contains the largest remaining populations of both species (National Research Council, 2004).

Life history and spawning characteristics of suckers in Upper Klamath Lake are reasonably well documented (Scoppettone and Vinyard, 1991; Moyle, 2002; Cooperman and Markle, 2003). Age estimates for Lost River suckers have exceeded 40 years, age estimates for shortnose suckers (SNS) have exceeded 30 years (National Research Council, 2004). Both species are obligate lake dwellers that make spawning migrations between March and May of each year. Shortnose suckers spawn primarily in the Williamson and Sprague Rivers, but two distinct subpopulations of Lost River suckers have been identified in Upper Klamath Lake (National Research Council, 2004). One subpopulation spawns in the Williamson and Sprague Rivers, and the other subpopulation spawns at several spring upwelling areas along the eastern shoreline of the lake below Modoc Rim (fig. 1). Capture-recapture data show an extremely high degree of spawning site fidelity and little reproductive mixing between the two subpopulations (Janney and others, 2008).

Although fishing mortality was eliminated with the closure of the recreational fishery in 1987, poor survival of adult suckers is still considered a factor limiting recovery of Upper Klamath Lake populations (Janney and others, 2008). Upper Klamath Lake has progressed to a hypereutrophic state due to increased nutrient loading from wetland drainage, grazing, and timber harvest (Bradbury and others, 2004; Eilers and others, 2004). These conditions lead to massive blooms of the cyanobacterium *Aphanizomenon flos-aquae* between June and October of each year (Kann and Smith, 1999; Wood and others, 2008; Lindenberg and others, 2009). The algal blooms and their subsequent die-offs produce water quality conditions that are deleterious to fish health—low concentrations of dissolved oxygen, elevated concentrations of ammonia, and high pH. Poor water quality conditions are thought to have contributed to a number of substantial fish die-offs in the lake, most recently during the summers of 1986, 1995, 1996, 1997 (National Research Council, 2004), and, to a much lesser extent, in the summer of 2003 (U.S. Geological Survey, unpub. data).

In this report, we summarize data collected in 2009 on the timing and magnitude of adult sucker spawning migrations and analyze capture-recapture data from 1999 to 2009 to evaluate demographic trends in LRS and SNS populations. Annual adult survival and recruitment were modeled and compared to assess differences attributable to species, LRS subpopulation, sex, and year. We used model-averaged estimates of these probabilities to calculate estimates of population rate of change. In addition to estimating recruitment from capture-recapture data, we assessed relative changes in size composition to provide additional insight into the relative frequency and magnitude of recruitment into the adult sucker populations.

Methods

Sampling and Fish Handling

The Lost River sucker subpopulation that spawns at spring upwelling areas along the eastern shoreline of Upper Klamath Lake was sampled at four locations (fig. 1) using 30 m trammel nets (1.8 m high; two 30 cm mesh outer panels; one 3.8 cm mesh inner panel; foam-core float line; lead-core bottom line). Nets were set twice per week at each spawning area (hereafter, spring) between February and May from 1999 to 2009. The only exception to this sampling schedule occurred in 2006, when each spring was sampled only once per week. Nets were set starting at the shoreline and extending out in a semicircular fashion, encompassing the area where spawning activity was concentrated.

Lost River and shortnose suckers also were sampled at two locations within tributary rivers. Between 2000 and 2008, fish were sampled three times per week at the Chiloquin Dam fish ladder on the Sprague River (fig. 1). Before sampling, a screen was placed over the bottom entrance (outflow) to prevent fish from exiting, and the upstream end (inflow) was blocked by a board to lower the water level in the cells of the fish ladder. A combination of dip nets and short trammel nets were then used to collect fish trapped in the ladder. Beginning in 2005 and continuing through 2009, a resistance board weir [described in detail by Tobin (1994)] was deployed on the Williamson River at river kilometer 10 to improve capture rates of suckers during the spawning migrations (fig. 1). The weir restricted the passage of suckers to two short sections, each fitted with a live trap. An upstream trap was used to capture fish as they migrated upriver, and a downstream trap was used to allow downriver migrating suckers to pass the weir. High flows in the Williamson River during most of the 2006 spawning season inundated the weir and allowed fish to pass over and around the weir without swimming through the trap.

Additional trammel net sampling for pre-spawn adult suckers of both species was conducted from 1995 to 2009 at various staging areas in Upper Klamath Lake. The overwhelming majority of this type of sampling in recent years has taken place near Modoc Point and Goose Bay (fig. 1). In addition, between 1995 and 2006, pre-spawn suckers were sampled with trammel nets in the lowest couple kilometers of the Williamson River (Janney and others, 2006).

Suckers captured at all sample locations were identified to species and sex, measured for fork length (FL), and scanned for the presence of a passive integrated transponder (PIT) tag. If a PIT tag was not detected, one was inserted into the ventral abdominal musculature anterior to the pelvic girdle. From 1995 to 2004, suckers were tagged with 125 kHz full-duplex (FDX) PIT tags. All tagging since the 2005 sampling season has used 134.2 kHz FDX tags. All fish were released soon after being tagged.

Remote Passive Integrated Transponder Tag Detection Systems

In addition to capture sampling, detections of PIT-tagged fish on remote antennas were incorporated into the capture-recapture study design beginning in 2005. Remote antennas were incorporated to improve the probability of re-encountering previously tagged suckers (Hewitt and others, 2010). Suckers detected by these systems were not physically handled, but were confirmed to be alive and thus were considered live recaptures in survival analyses. Locations of remote PIT tag detection systems are shown in figure 1, and are listed here with the range of years during which they were operational:

- antennas on the substrate at lakeshore springs in Upper Klamath Lake (2005–2009);
- one antenna in each of the upstream and downstream traps of the Williamson River weir (2005–2009);
- a river-wide antenna array on the substrate immediately upstream of the weir (2007–2009);
- an antenna array on the substrate immediately downstream of the Chiloquin Dam site (2008–2009);
- antennas in the entrance, middle, and exit of the Chiloquin Dam fish ladder (2006–2008);
- a river-wide antenna array on the substrate about 2.5 river kilometers upstream of the Chiloquin Dam site (2007–2009); and
- a river-wide antenna array on the substrate about 12 river kilometers upstream of the Chiloquin Dam site at Braymill (2008–2009).

Survival Analysis

We used Cormack-Jolly-Seber (CJS) live-recapture models (Williams and others, 2002; Nichols, 2005) to obtain maximum likelihood estimates of apparent survival (Φ) and recapture (p) probabilities. Apparent survival is the complement of the sum of mortality and permanent emigration (Pollock and others, 2007), but radio telemetry data indicate that permanent emigration out of Upper Klamath Lake and its tributaries by either sucker species is rare (Banish and others, 2009). Therefore, we expect that our estimates of apparent survival are nearly equivalent to true survival. Lost River sucker data were analyzed separately for the two spawning subpopulations (lakeshore spawners and river spawners). Captures of Lost River suckers in Upper Klamath Lake outside of the spawning areas were excluded from analyses because the subpopulation membership of those fish could not be determined.

The CJS model makes the following assumptions: (1) tags are not lost, or missed when individuals are re-encountered; (2) sampling periods are "instantaneous" relative to the interval between samples; and (3) there is no unmodeled individual variability (heterogeneity) in survival or encounter probabilities among the tagged individuals. Although double-tagging experiments with Floy and PIT tags showed that PIT tag loss rates were less than 1 percent over 3 or more years (U.S. Geological Survey, unpub. data), an unknown proportion of the 125 kHz PIT tags released in 2001–2003 are not detectable on the remote antennas. For physical recaptures, we ensured that tags were not missed when present by scanning a test tag prior to scanning each fish, and also scanning a test tag after each fish that was found to be untagged. Regarding Assumption 2, sampling in our study occurs over a 3–3.5 month spawning period and is not instantaneous. However, the vast majority of captures and encounters occur over a much shorter time period, and individuals are fairly consistent from year to year in the relative times at which they join the spawning aggregation. Thus, on an individual basis, sampling can be considered nearly instantaneous relative to an annual interval used for parameter estimation. In addition, spawning fish almost always appear to be in excellent condition and water quality is good during the spring. Thus, we expect that little mortality occurs during the sampling period and does not bias survival estimates.

We assessed whether our data conformed to the assumptions of the CJS model using goodness-of-fit testing in the program U-CARE (Choquet and others, 2009). Goodness-of-fit tests pooled over time indicated significant departures from frequencies expected under the CJS model for Lost River sucker subpopulations and for shortnose suckers. Lack of fit can be an indication of model assumption violations, sparse data, or lack of independence. Closer examination of our goodness-of-fit tests for individual time periods revealed no consistent or systematic bias that would suggest tagging effects. Lack of fit in our data probably was due to a combination of sparse recaptures at the beginning of the study and lack of independence. The lack of independence, or overdispersion, probably results from schooling behavior and is relatively common in capture-recapture studies of schooling fish (Pollock and others, 2007). An overdispersion correction factor ($\hat{c}$) was determined from the most general model for each species or subpopulation by use of the median $\hat{c}$ estimation method in program MARK (Cooch and White, 2010). These $\hat{c}$ values were applied to the respective set of candidate models to compensate for overdispersion in model selection statistics and to inflate variances associated with parameter estimates. Applying a variance inflation factor is recommended when heterogeneity is detected in the data, and supports a conservative approach to inference based on model selection (Anderson and others, 1994).

Model sets were developed by considering the effects of sex and time (year) on Φ and p, and then including models with and without those factors. We modeled Φ as a function of sex because past analyses have shown that female suckers often have higher survival than males (Janney and others, 2008; Hewitt and others, 2010). Most importantly, we modeled Φ as a function of time to detect changes in annual survival. For p, we expected sex to be important because of differences in reproductive behavior (for example, males stay at spawning areas longer than females, potentially increasing their probability of being encountered), and we expected time to be important because of annual differences in sampling intensity and environmental effects on the condition of the spawning habitat. Past analyses showed that models with some combination of both sex and time effects on p were overwhelmingly supported in model selection, so we only considered models with some combination of both effects (Janney and others, 2008). We included models with both additive and interactive effects for Φ and p. Additive models constrained effects to be the same between groups across time (for example, the difference between male and female survival is the same in each year), whereas interactive models included more parameters and allowed effects to vary through time (for example, separate estimates of survival for each sex in each year). Note that, as in many CJS designs, the last estimates of Φ and p are confounded in the likelihood and cannot be separately estimated. As such, we do not report or discuss estimates of Φ for 2008 or p for 2009.

The models used in the analysis were specified and passed to program MARK (White and Burnham, 1999) using the RMark package (Laake, 2010; Laake and Rexstad, 2010) within the R software environment (R Development Core Team, 2010). All model likelihoods were constructed using a logit link function and optimized using the default Newton-Raphson algorithm. We used Akaike's information criterion corrected for small sample bias and adjusted for overdispersion (quasilikelihood AICc, or QAICc) as a statistical criterion to evaluate the competing models (Burnham and Anderson,

2002). Akaike weights (w_i) are reported as a measure of the relative weight among the models, or the likelihood of each model being the best model in the set given the data. Rather than making inferences from only the best model in the set, the one with the smallest QAICc value, parameter estimates were model-averaged using the w_i as weights. Model-averaged parameter estimates account for model selection uncertainty in the estimated precision of the parameters and thus produce unconditional estimates of variances and standard errors (Buckland and others, 1997).

Recruitment and Population Rate of Change

A primary requirement for recovering the endangered sucker populations is knowledge of changes in population size over time. In addition to survival, recruitment can be estimated from open population capture-recapture data (Pradel, 1996; Franklin, 2001; Nichols, 2005). Specifically, the reverse-time analog of survival can be estimated; this parameter is termed seniority and denoted γ. Seniority is defined as the probability that an animal present in the sampled population at period i was also present in period i-1. Given estimates of Φ and γ, population rate of change ($\lambda_i = N_{i+1}/N_i$), can be estimated without estimating N using the equation:

$$\lambda_i = \frac{\Phi_i}{\gamma_{i+1}}$$

Pradel (1996) introduced a likelihood that models the entire encounter history and is based on the temporal symmetry of capture-recapture data (Nichols and Hines, 2002). This approach combines probabilities describing forward time (survival) and reverse-time (seniority) processes, allowing the direct estimation and modeling of λ. The assumptions of the temporal symmetry model are similar to those in the Cormack-Jolly-Seber model, but temporal symmetry further assumes that the study area is well defined and does not expand over time and that there is no permanent trap response in capture probability. The incorporation of remote PIT tag detection systems into our study design in 2005 created a situation in which previously tagged fish have a much greater probability of being re-encountered than untagged fish have of being captured in trammel nets. In essence, the remote antenna systems create a dramatic "trap-happy" response in capture probability (Otis and others, 1978). This difference in capture probabilities does not cause bias in survival estimates from CJS models, but it does cause substantial bias in estimates of seniority and population rate of change from temporal symmetry models (Hines and Nichols, 2002).

To avoid such bias, we obtained estimates of survival and seniority from separate model sets and then used the estimates to calculate λ with the equation given above. Encounter histories used to model survival included physical captures and remote detections, but seniority models included only physical captures. Early estimates of γ are not reported because of poor precision due to sparse data and because simulations have shown that the initial two γ estimates are likely to be substantially more biased than subsequent estimates (Hines and Nichols, 2002). Model sets for the seniority analyses were developed and evaluated in a way similar to the survival analyses; however, effects of tag type on p were not included in models for seniority because remote detections were not included. Standard errors for the derived estimates of λ were calculated using the Delta method. Ideally, estimates of survival and seniority would be generated from a single likelihood using a temporal symmetry model (Pradel, 1996), and the standard error for λ estimates would be corrected for the covariance between these two parameters. Our calculation of the standard error of λ by the Delta method ignores the covariance between survival and seniority. The effect of this approach on the estimated standard errors is expected to be small, but the presented standard errors for λ may be too precise.

Annual estimates of λ provide insight into the variability in abundance and the health of adult spawning populations by showing whether the population decreased ($\lambda < 1$), remained stable ($\lambda = 1$), or increased ($\lambda > 1$). We summarize the long-term dynamics of the populations using a quantity known as Δ_t, which is simply the cumulative product of the λ estimates over a time period of interest (Anthony and others, 2006). This quantity describes the percentage change in population size from the beginning of the period to the end. Values of Δ_t greater than 1.0 (100 percent) indicate increases in population size and values less than 1.0 indicate decreases in population size. We emphasize that estimates of λ and Δ_t values apply only to the adult spawning populations and are not necessarily representative of changes in the whole populations. Increases in juvenile abundance are not incorporated until those individuals join the spawning aggregations and are fully vulnerable to our sampling. Size composition of the catches in the most recent year, described next, may provide an earlier indication of potential recruitment.

Size Composition Analysis

Fork lengths of captured suckers were used to assess changes in the size structure of the LRS subpopulations and the SNS population over time. This assessment corroborates evidence of recruitment, or the lack thereof, from capture-recapture seniority estimates, and also illustrates trends in growth. Length data were grouped separately for each sex within each population or subpopulation, and we calculated an average annual growth rate for each group by fitting a simple linear regression to the successive medians of the annual length distributions. Data from 1999 to 2009 were included for the lakeshore spawning subpopulation of LRS, and data from 2000 to 2009 were included for the river spawning subpopulation of LRS and for SNS.

For the lakeshore spawning subpopulation of LRS and for SNS, length analyses and capture-recapture analyses are focused on the same statistical populations. In contrast, for the river spawning subpopulation of LRS, the two analyses are focused on different statistical populations. In order to focus only on spawning adults, the capture-recapture analysis is restricted to fish that were encountered in either the Williamson River or Sprague River during at least one spawning season and that were never encountered at the lakeshore springs. Many LRS are captured during sampling in Upper Klamath Lake outside of the spawning areas, and these individuals do not enter our capture-recapture analyses until they are encountered at a spawning area (lakeshore springs or one of the rivers). In contrast, the length analysis for the river spawning subpopulation includes all LRS that were never encountered at the lakeshore springs, including fish captured in Upper Klamath Lake that were never encountered at a spawning area. As a result, the length analysis may include data for small LRS that are not yet mature but are staging with the spawners in the lake prior to the spawning migration. This is done intentionally to provide an early indication of recruitment to the spawning subpopulation, if and when recruitment occurs.

Results

Lost River Suckers

Catch Summary and Run Timing for 2009

We captured 1,419 LRS in trammel nets at the lakeshore springs, 638 (45 percent) of which had been tagged prior to the 2009 sampling season (table 1). Trammel net catches at the springs began in mid-March and continued through late May (fig. 2). The majority of individuals were first captured at Cinder Flats (40 percent) or Sucker Springs (39 percent), followed by Silver Building Springs and Ouxy Springs (11 percent each). One female was captured at Silver Building Springs that had not been captured since it was originally Floy-tagged by the Klamath Tribes at Chiloquin Dam in 1988. The fish had grown 258 mm in 21 years, from 463 mm FL to 721 mm FL. In addition to the fish physically captured in trammel nets, 6,056 PIT-tagged LRS were detected swimming over remote antennas at the lakeshore springs. Antennas at Sucker Springs detected more individuals than antennas at any other spring (table 2). Lost River suckers were detected beginning in the last week of February and continued to be detected until the antennas were removed during the last week of May (fig. 3). Most individuals joined the spawning aggregation in April. At the lakeshore springs, only 20 percent of the LRS detected on the remote antennas also were physically captured in trammel nets, whereas 84 percent of the PIT-tagged LRS that were physically captured also were detected on the remote antennas.

Trammel net sampling at pre-spawn staging areas captured 1,569 individual LRS (table 1). Of these, 209 (13 percent) had been tagged prior to the 2009 sampling season. Of the PIT-tagged LRS captured at the staging areas, 83 percent were subsequently captured or detected somewhere in the Williamson or Sprague Rivers, whereas only 5 percent were later captured or detected at the lakeshore springs. Three individuals were subsequently captured or detected at both spawning areas.

A total of 3,279 LRS were captured in the upstream trap of the Williamson River weir; only 271 (8 percent) had been tagged prior to 2009 (table 1). Most individuals were captured in mid- to late April (fig. 4). The combination of remote PIT tag antennas at the weir (upstream and downstream traps and the river-wide array) detected a total of 12,509 individuals (table 2). The antenna on the upstream trap showed an increase in detections of new individuals on April 11 when water temperatures rose and approached 10 °C (fig. 5). Detections of new individuals declined when water temperatures decreased, but peaked again from April 17–23 when water temperatures rose and exceeded 10 °C.

Moving upstream from the Williamson River weir, the river-wide antenna array in the Sprague River just downstream of the Chiloquin Dam site detected 3,769 individual LRS between March 11 and the end of May (table 2). Most individuals were detected in mid- to late April when water temperatures were equal to or greater than 10 °C (fig. 6). The next upstream antenna array, located upstream of the Chiloquin Dam site, detected 901 LRS between March 12 and May 21. The farthest upstream array on the Sprague River, located at Braymill, detected 83 individual LRS between March 13 and May 23.

Survival, Recruitment, and Size Composition

Upper Klamath Lake Lakeshore Spawning Subpopulation

From 1999 to 2008, we captured, tagged, and released 3,538 female and 5,412 male Lost River suckers at the lakeshore springs. Excluding re-encounters in the year of tagging, we subsequently recaptured or remotely detected 2,955 (84 percent) of the females and 3,963 (73 percent) of the males on at least one occasion through 2009. An additional 191 females and 249 males from this subpopulation were re-encountered at the springs between 1999 and 2008 and also were included in the survival analysis.

Thirty-five CJS models were fitted to the encounter histories of fish in this subpopulation to estimate apparent annual survival and re-encounter probabilities. The top two models in the set had nearly equal weight (w_i = 0.37 and 0.35) and together accounted for the vast majority of the weight in the model set (table 3). The top two models differed only in the structure for the survival parameters. The best model included an additive effect of sex and year for Φ, and sex, year, and tag type effects for p. The second best model included separate Φ parameters for each sex in each year (a fully interactive model) and the same structure for p as in the best model. Model-averaged estimates of Φ varied across years and female survival was consistently, albeit only slightly, higher than male survival (fig. 7). With the exception of 2002, survival estimates were within the range expected for animals with a lifespan similar to that of Lost River suckers.

The encounter histories for the recruitment analysis included the same individuals as the survival analysis, but only included physical captures. As a result, the density of the encounter histories and the size of the model set were much reduced (10 models were initially considered). Model selection statistics indicated that the best model (w_i = 0.63) included only a single, time- and sex-constant parameter for seniority (γ). The second best model (w_i = 0.25) included an effect of sex on γ, but the difference between the sexes in the estimates from that model was trivial (< 0.01). The remaining models in the set that had any support ($w_i \leq 0.08$) included a time effect on γ. However, many of the γ estimates in these models were on the boundary at 1.0, indicating estimability problems. As a result, these models (6) had to be removed from the set used to generate model-averaged estimates of γ. The final model-averaged estimates of γ were high (γ = 0.97 for both sexes, SE $\approx$ 0.01), indicating very little recruitment of new individuals into the adult spawning population. Because these estimates of seniority were higher than estimates of apparent survival in every year between 2002 and 2007, the derived estimates of population rate of change (λ) were always less than 1.0 (fig. 7). Compounding the λ estimates across this 6-year period suggests that the abundance of female LRS in this subpopulation declined by 25 percent (Δ_t = 0.75), and the abundance of male LRS declined by 44 percent (Δ_t = 0.56).

Given the number of γ estimates that were on the boundary at 1.0 in seniority models that included time effects, and the fork length data collected over the last decade, we consider the overall estimates of population decline given above to be lower bounds (that is, the declines may be more substantial than these estimates indicate). Although models with time effects on γ had little weight in model selection, the boundary estimates in those models indicate that in some years γ may be even closer to 1.0 than the model-averaged estimates indicate (γ = 0.97). Indeed, the length data show that very few individuals of either sex collected since 1999 could be considered new recruits to the spawning population (fig. 8). A difference of a few percent in estimates of γ seems trivial, but such differences can be important in terms of the overall Δ_t when compounded across 6 years. We calculated what we consider to be upper bounds on the overall declines by allowing γ to be 1.0 in all years ($\lambda = \Phi$). These calculations indicate that the decline for females could be as much as 38 percent ($\Delta_t = 0.62$) and the decline for males could be as much as 53 percent ($\Delta_t = 0.47$).

 A more complete time series of fork length data was given in Janney and others (2008), and showed that this subpopulation "turned over" during the early to mid-1990s. Prior to 1990, the subpopulation was rather homogeneous and was composed of relatively old, large individuals (males ≈ 650 mm FL; females ≈ 725 mm FL). Recruitment in the late 1980s to early 1990s, coupled with substantial losses of adults in large fish die-offs in 1995, 1996, and 1997, resulted in relatively young and small populations in the late 1990s and early 2000s. It appears that this subpopulation is now composed of a subset of the same individuals that were present in the early 2000s. Over the most recent decade, both sexes grew at consistent rates across years, with females adding about 12 mm FL per year and males about 10 mm FL per year (fig. 8). At present, the median fork length of males is 628 mm and the median fork length of females is 685 mm, and individuals of both sexes show relatively little variability in size.

Williamson and Sprague River Spawning Subpopulation

 From 2000 to 2008, we captured, tagged, and released 6,595 female and 4,177 male Lost River suckers in the Williamson River or the Sprague River. Excluding re-encounters in the year of tagging, we subsequently recaptured or remotely detected 5,407 (82 percent) of the females and 3,200 (77 percent) of the males on at least one occasion through 2009. An additional 1,934 females and 1,583 males from this subpopulation were re-encountered in one of the rivers between 2000 and 2008 and also were included in the survival analysis. Almost all of these additional individuals were fish originally captured, tagged, and released at pre-spawn staging areas in Upper Klamath Lake.

 Model selection statistics for the 35 CJS models fitted to the encounter histories for this subpopulation indicated that the most parameterized model received nearly all of the support ($w_i = 0.91$; table 4). The model included separate survival (Φ) parameters for each sex in each year, separate re-encounter probabilities (p) for each sex in each year, and separate tag type effects on p for each sex in year from 2006 to 2009. The second best model ($w_i = 0.07$) was the same as the top model except that it included a less complex additive effect of sex and year for Φ. Model-averaged estimates of Φ showed that survival varied over time for this subpopulation more than for the lakeshore spawning subpopulation (fig. 9). Survival of both sexes in 2000 was low, with female survival (0.83) higher than that for males (0.64). The estimates for males in 2001 and both sexes in 2004 were on the boundary at 1.0, indicating estimability problems, and the estimates for females in 2001 and males in 2005 were high but imprecise. Given the precision of the remaining estimates, survival for both sexes was high and similar to each other in 2002, 2003, 2005, and 2007. Survival of females in 2006 was similar to the other years, but male survival was substantially lower in 2006 (0.81). With the exception of the year 2000 and males in 2006, survival of both sexes was similar to estimates from the lakeshore spawning subpopulation.

 The encounter histories and modeling for the recruitment analysis were handled in the same way as for the lakeshore spawning subpopulation. Model selection statistics indicated that the best model included an additive effect of sex and year on seniority (γ), and this model accounted for more than one-half of the weight ($w_i = 0.68$). Parameter estimates from this model showed about a 5 percent difference in γ between the sexes, indicating more recruitment for males than for females. The second best model included only an effect of year on γ, and this model received almost all of the remaining weight ($w_i = 0.26$). All of the models in the set that received any support included year effects on seniority, but the γ

estimates in these models for all years except 2003 ($\gamma \approx 0.73$) and 2006 ($\gamma \approx 0.35$) were estimated on the boundary at 1.0. As in the analysis for the lakeshore spawning subpopulation, these models (6) had to be removed from the set used to generate model-averaged estimates of γ. Thus, the final estimates are sex-specific but time-constant: $\gamma = 0.76$ (SE = 0.02) for females; $\gamma = 0.74$ (SE = 0.02) for males.

The model-averaged estimates of seniority given above indicate that, in each year between 2002 and 2007, approximately 25 percent of the individuals of each sex in this subpopulation were newly recruited to the spawning population. However, the fork length data collected over the last decade shows that few individuals were new recruits in any of those years (fig. 10). The low estimates of seniority probably are biased by an important assumption violation related to how we sampled the river spawning subpopulation over time. In particular, sampling in the Chiloquin Dam fish ladder in 2006, aided by extremely high flows in that year, provided access to large numbers of fish that had been previously unavailable to our sampling. These individuals are erroneously represented in the seniority estimates as new recruits. A key assumption of reverse-time capture-recapture models, which this change in sampling violates, is that the sampling frame does not expand over time (Hines and Nichols 2002). Essentially, sampling at the fish ladder in 2006 acted as a major 1-year expansion of the sampling frame. The effect on our analysis is that seniority models with time effects are strongly supported despite their estimation problems. Those models receive support because estimates of γ in 2006 are so low and contrast so strongly with the estimates in all other years. Even though the model-averaged estimates given above do not include estimates of γ from time-specific models, the time-constant estimates from the remaining simpler models are "pulled down" to account for the 2006 data. As a result, the model-averaged estimates of γ are not reliable and cannot be used to calculate λ and Δ_t. Similar to the lakeshore spawning subpopulation, we provide upper bounds on the overall declines of males and females in this subpopulation by calculating Δ_t allowing γ to be 1.0 in all years ($\lambda = \Phi$). Recall that the estimates of γ for all years other than 2003 and 2006 in the time-specific models were on the boundary at 1.0. Although this indicates problems with estimation, the length data indicate that it is entirely reasonable that there was no recruitment of new individuals in those years. Although we have no reason to discount the low estimates of γ in 2003 (0.76 for females and 0.71 for males) because of sampling, the length data indicate that recruitment on the order of 25 percent for either sex in that year also is suspect. Over the 6-year period from 2002 to 2007, the abundance of females in this subpopulation may have declined by as much as 33 percent ($\Delta_t = 0.67$) and the abundance of males may have declined by as much as 39 percent ($\Delta_t = 0.61$).

The time series of fork length data provided in Janney and others (2008) showed that the river spawning subpopulation of LRS went through a demographic transition similar to that experienced by the lakeshore spawning subpopulation. In the mid-1980s, this subpopulation was rather homogeneous and was composed of relatively old, large individuals (males $\approx$ 620 mm FL; females $\approx$ 675 mm FL), although somewhat smaller than individuals in the lakeshore spawning subpopulation. As a result of recruitment in the late 1980s to early 1990s, and losses of adults in fish die-offs in 1995, 1996, and 1997, the subpopulation was composed of relatively young and small individuals by the late 1990s. A subset of those individuals apparently now makes up the current spawning population. Over the most recent decade, both sexes grew at consistent rates across years, with females adding about 11 mm FL per year and males about 8 mm FL per year (fig. 10). At present, the median fork length of males is 598 mm and the median fork length of females is 650 mm. In general, individuals of both sexes show relatively little variability in size. Although some small fish collected at pre-spawn staging areas are evident in some years (for example, females in 2004), these smaller fish never make up a substantial portion of the sample.

Shortnose Suckers

Catch Summary and Run Timing for 2009

Trammel net sampling at lakeshore springs captured 10 individual shortnose suckers, six of which had been tagged prior to the 2009 sampling season (table 1). All four of the newly tagged individuals were females. Two of them stayed at the springs for an extended period of time, one was detected at the Williamson River weir throughout May, and the other was not re-encountered in 2009. In total, the remote PIT tag antennas at the lakeshore springs detected 44 individual SNS, and more individuals were detected at Sucker Springs than at any other spring (table 2). The vast majority of detections occurred during May. Of the 44 individuals detected, 11 (25 percent) also were captured or detected in the Williamson or Sprague Rivers in 2009, and a total of 16 (36 percent) have been captured or detected in one of the rivers in the past. For the lakeshore springs as a whole, only 8 of the 44 (18 percent) SNS detected on the remote PIT tag antennas also were captured in trammel nets, whereas 8 of the 10 (80 percent) SNS captured in trammel nets also were detected on the remote PIT tag antennas.

We captured 1,794 shortnose suckers in trammel nets at pre-spawn staging areas; 452 (25 percent) of these individuals had been tagged prior to the 2009 sampling season (table 1). Of the PIT-tagged SNS captured at the staging areas, 75 percent were subsequently captured or detected somewhere in the Williamson or Sprague Rivers. Only 3 individuals were later captured or detected at the lakeshore springs.

A total of 368 SNS were captured in the upstream trap of the Williamson River weir, and 81 (25 percent) had been tagged prior to the 2009 sampling season. Most individuals were captured between late April and early May. The remote PIT tag antennas at the weir combined to detect a total of 5,023 individual SNS (table 2). One individual, a male, was PIT-tagged and released in Lake Ewauna on April 22, passed through the Link River Dam fish ladder on May 20, and arrived at the weir on May 25. Nearly one-half (2,458) of the individuals detected on a remote antenna at or near the weir were detected by the antenna on the upstream trap. Three peaks occurred in detections of SNS on the upstream trap antenna (fig. 11). The first two peaks coincided with the peaks in LRS detections on April 11 and April 17–23, although the magnitudes of the peaks were reversed compared to those for LRS with more detections occurring in the later peak. The largest peak in detections of SNS occurred on May 8–9 when temperatures were rising and exceeding 12 °C. The weir and its associated traps were removed on May 21, so some of the detections on the river-wide array after this date were likely of fish moving back downstream after spawning.

The PIT tag antenna array in the Sprague River downstream of the Chiloquin Dam site detected 827 individual SNS (table 2). The vast majority of detections occurred during May when water temperatures were near or greater than 12 °C. The antenna array upstream of the Chiloquin Dam site detected 447 SNS, and the antenna array at Braymill detected 18.

Survival, Recruitment, and Size Composition

Between 1999 and 2008, we captured, tagged, and released 7,491 female and 4,172 male shortnose suckers. Excluding re-encounters in the year of tagging, we subsequently recaptured or remotely detected 4,563 (61 percent) of the females and 2,311 (55 percent) of the males on at least one occasion through 2009. An additional 212 females and 149 males were re-encountered between 1999 and 2008 and also were included in the survival analysis.

Thirty-five CJS models were fitted to the SNS encounter histories to estimate apparent annual survival and re-encounter probabilities. The top model in the set had all of the weight (table 5). The model included separate Φ parameters for each sex in each year, as well as additive sex and year effects for p and separate tag type effects for p in each year from 2006 to 2009. Model-averaged estimates of Φ showed that survival was similar between the sexes in most years, but female survival was substantially higher than male survival in 2002 and 2006 (fig. 12). Survival for both sexes was especially low in 2001 and 2004. With the exception of those years, survival estimates were similar to estimates for Lost River suckers and were within the range expected for animals with a lifespan similar to that of shortnose suckers.

The encounter histories and modeling for the recruitment analysis were handled in the same way as for Lost River suckers. Model selection statistics indicated that the best model included an additive effect of sex and year on seniority (γ), and this model accounted for nearly all of the weight ($w_i = 0.92$). However, the difference in estimates of γ between the sexes from this model was small (< 0.02). The second best model included only an effect of year on γ, but this model had little weight ($w_i = 0.07$). These two models were the only ones in the set that had any support, but the γ estimates in these models for all years except 2006 were estimated on the boundary at 1.0. As a result, these models were removed from the set used to generate model-averaged estimates of γ. The final estimates are sex-specific but time-constant: $\gamma = 0.90$ (SE = 0.02) for females; $\gamma = 0.92$ (SE = 0.01) for males. Estimates of apparent survival and seniority were similar for males in 2003, females in 2006, and both sexes in 2007, yielding derived estimates of λ close to 1.0 in those years (fig. 12). For all other years, estimates of seniority were higher than apparent survival and derived estimates of λ were less than 1.0, with the smallest values occurring in 2001 and 2004. Compounding the λ estimates over the 7-year period from 2001 to 2007 suggests that the abundance of female SNS declined by 52 percent ($\Delta_t = 0.48$) and the abundance of male SNS declined by 58 percent ($\Delta_t = 0.42$).

Similar to lakeshore spawning Lost River suckers, the decline in the population could be greater than these estimates indicate. The model-averaged estimates of seniority suggest that about 10 percent of the individuals in the population were new recruits in each year between 2001 and 2007. However, the fork length data provide strong evidence that few individuals were new recruits in any of those years (fig. 13). The same sampling issue that caused bias in the recruitment analysis for the river spawning subpopulation of LRS, the sampling of fish in the Chiloquin Dam fish ladder in 2006, also caused bias in the recruitment analysis for the SNS population. Seniority models with time effects are strongly supported, despite estimation problems, because the data appear to indicate substantial recruitment in 2006. In that year, the estimates of γ from the model with the most support, the one that included an additive effect of sex and year on γ, were 0.78 (SE = 0.04) for females and 0.63 (SE = 0.05) for males. Furthermore, although the model-averaged estimates given above do not include estimates of γ from time-specific models, the model-averaged estimates are "pulled down" to account for the data in 2006. We provide upper bounds on the overall declines of SNS by re-calculating Δ_t for each sex allowing γ to be 1.0 in all years. Given that the estimates of γ for all years other than 2006 in the time-specific models were on the boundary at 1.0, and that the length data provide little evidence of recruitment in any year, these upper bounds are entirely reasonable. Indeed, we consider these upper bounds to be more realistic descriptors of the status of shortnose suckers. The decline for females could be as much as 73 percent ($\Delta_t = 0.27$) and the decline for males could be as much as 80 percent ($\Delta_t = 0.20$).

The more complete time series of fork length data provided in Janney and others (2008) showed that the shortnose sucker population in Upper Klamath Lake experienced a demographic transition similar to that for Lost River suckers. In the mid-1980s, the SNS population was rather homogeneous and was composed of relatively old and large individuals (males ≈ 425 mm FL; females ≈ 450 mm FL). The population then "turned over" as a result of recruitment in the late 1980s to early 1990s and losses of adults in fish die-offs in 1995, 1996, and 1997. The current population is mostly a subset of the individuals that were present in the late 1990s. Over the most recent decade, both sexes grew at consistent rates across years, adding about 5 mm FL per year. At present, the median fork length of each sex is similar to what it was in the mid-1980s (males = 427 mm FL; females = 452 mm), and individuals of both sexes show little variability in size.

Discussion

Continuing declines in the size of the spawning populations of Lost River and shortnose suckers in Upper Klamath Lake, primarily due to lack of recruitment, are cause for serious concern. Both subpopulations of LRS have declined less than the population of SNS, but the abundance of both species has declined substantially over the last decade. As a result, the sucker populations in Upper Klamath Lake remain at risk of extirpation from catastrophic events, such as the fish die-offs in the mid-1990s that removed thousands of individuals from the populations of both species (Perkins and others, 2000).

With the exception of just a few years, the survival of spawning adult Lost River suckers in both subpopulations has typically been high and in line with expectations for an animal with an average lifespan of 25+ years. In contrast to earlier conclusions (Janney and others, 2008, 2009), current analyses indicate that survival generally is similar between the two subpopulations of LRS, with a few exceptions (both sexes in 2000 and males in 2006). The large amount of re-encounter data obtained in recent years from the remote PIT tag detection systems has led to model selection results that favor more complex models and has refined survival estimates, particularly for the river spawning subpopulation. For example, Janney and others (2008) showed that survival was particularly low for the river spawning subpopulation in 2002 (≈ 0.65). In contrast, current estimates show that survival for both sexes in that subpopulation in 2002 was about 0.90. In addition, precision on all survival estimates has improved over time, although precision in all but the most recent years for river spawning LRS and SNS is still poorer than for lakeshore spawning LRS. As demonstrated in Hewitt and others (2010), the remote detection systems have greatly increased the amount of information about survival contained in the encounter histories. Previously, fish could elude capture for many years and their fates would be erroneously interpreted as mortalities in survival models. Now, with high re-encounter probabilities, large numbers of these fish have been re-encountered on the remote detection systems and their histories properly show that they were alive but were not being captured. In addition to improving our time series of survival estimates, the remote detection systems also will allow future analyses to investigate the roles that various factors play in sucker population dynamics (for example, water quality or disease).

Despite relatively low annual mortality for Lost River suckers, mortality compounded over many years without addition of new individuals from recruitment has resulted in considerable declines in abundance. The numbers of spawning adults of both sexes in both LRS subpopulations probably have declined by more than 30 percent since 2002, and males in the lakeshore spawning subpopulation may have declined by more than 50 percent. Nonetheless, our monitoring efforts in 2009 showed that more than 6,000 PIT-tagged LRS were present in the spawning aggregations at the lakeshore springs, and only 45 percent of the individuals that were captured in trammel nets at the springs were already PIT-tagged (that is, had been handled by us in a previous year). Similarly, we encountered more than 12,500 LRS from the river spawning subpopulation in 2009, and less than 10 percent of those captured in the Williamson River weir were already tagged.

The current status of the shortnose sucker population is more dire. The number of spawning adults of both sexes has declined by more than 50 percent since 2001, and the declines probably are more than 70 percent after considering estimation problems in the capture-recapture recruitment analysis. Our 2009 sampling yielded encounters with just over 5,000 PIT-tagged SNS, and 25 percent of the individuals captured in the Williamson River weir were already tagged. Survival of both sexes was lower in 2001 and 2004 than would be expected for a species with the longevity of SNS.

Survival of both species, but especially of SNS, was low in the mid-1990s, coincident with the large fish die-offs that occurred in those years (Janney and others, 2008). However, low annual survival in the last decade has occurred in years when no fish die-offs were observed (for example, SNS in 2004, male river spawning LRS in 2006), and survival has been high in years with poor summer water quality when fish die-offs were observed (for example, 2003; Wood and others, 2006). In general, conspicuous fish die-offs are not necessarily reliable indicators of low annual survival.

Our capture-recapture analyses of recruitment and the derived estimates of the declines in abundance of spawners are vexed by a few important issues. First, because estimates of seniority must be based on data sets that include only physical captures, the amount of data available to estimate seniority is far less than that available for estimating survival. As a result, we often encounter estimation problems, such as boundary estimates of seniority (1.0), and model selection results that are less straightforward than for survival models. We must rely on various sources of information to properly interpret results of recruitment analyses, particularly if and when recruitment occurs in the future. Our comprehensive capture sampling yields detailed information on size composition that provides an important comparison with capture-recapture estimates of seniority. For example, boundary estimates of seniority are partly due to data sparseness, but also are reasonable given the apparent dearth of recruitment that is illustrated by the time series of size composition data. We are essentially trying to estimate something that does not exist, which causes problems for the numerical routines used to find the maximum of the model likelihood functions. These issues are less troublesome for the lakeshore spawning subpopulation of LRS from an interpretation standpoint, but are nonetheless important for interpreting all capture-recapture analyses of recruitment. For each population, we have provided our best interpretation and calculated estimates of Δ_t that should bound the true trajectory of abundance. The second important issue is the assumption violation related to sampling of the Chiloquin Dam fish ladder in 2006. This violation will remain a source of bias in all recruitment analyses for SNS and river spawning LRS. Essentially, we will have to ignore the "evidence" for recruitment in 2006 when calculating Δ_t for these populations, as we have done in this report. Finally, there is some potential for negative bias in survival estimates for the early 2000s. Some proportion of the 125 kHz PIT tags put out in 2001–2003 is not detectable by the remote PIT tag antennas. Although the extent of this problem is not yet known, negative bias in survival estimates would lead to negative bias in estimates of λ (that is, we would conclude that declines in abundance were greater than they really were).

The time series of fork length data for the two species indicates that current populations in Upper Klamath Lake are made up almost entirely of individuals spawned in the late 1980s and early 1990s. Given that nearly all of the individuals in the lake should be sexually mature, and the median size of the individuals in all populations has increased steadily over the last decade (SNS $\approx$ 5 mm per year; LRS $\approx$ 10 mm per year), our data contradict the conclusion that growth of these species in Upper Klamath Lake is determinate and essentially nonexistent several years after reproductive maturity (Terwilliger and others, 2010). The growth curves estimated by Terwilliger and others (2010) probably are inaccurate because they were based on samples of fish that were not collected in a way that was representative of the populations as a whole. For example, the SNS sample used by Terwilliger and others (2010) was clearly biased towards smaller individuals relative to the population as a whole [compare their figure 3 with figure 15 in Janney and others (2009)]. To illustrate the effects on the growth curves, we compared their estimates of asymptotic fork length (L_∞) from von Bertalanffy growth models to the sizes of fish from our sampling in spring 2009. They reported estimates of L_∞ for SNS of 425 mm FL for males and 464 mm FL for females. For comparison, the current median sizes of SNS are 427 mm FL for males and 452 mm FL for females. Data from the last few years indicates that there may be some slowing down of growth, but growth would have to completely stop in the next couple of years for their growth curve to accurately represent the trajectory in the current population. We consider it more reasonable that individuals in the current population will continue to grow and achieve sizes similar to those of adults present in the late 1980s. Comparisons for LRS are similar, although the size of fish in the two subpopulations is different and Terwilliger and others (2010) do not estimate growth curves separately for the subpopulations. Another important conclusion that is affected by the non-representative sampling relates to the relative strength of year classes. Terwilliger and others (2010) report that a strong year class occurred in 1998 for SNS (their figure 11). However, our data for this population as a whole shows that any contribution from the 1998 year class was trivial.

Acknowledgments

We thank Amari Dolan-Caret, Ryan Braham, Nicholas Miller, and Greta Blackwood for their dedication to the project and their assistance with data curation and management. David R. Anderson and Jeff Laake continue to provide valuable advice regarding data analysis. We thank Scott VanderKooi (USGS), John Beeman (USGS), and Josh Rasmussen (USFWS) for reviewing drafts of this report. Funding was provided by the Bureau of Reclamation, U.S. Department of Interior (Interagency Agreement 06AA204052) and USGS. Funding was provided by Reclamation as part of its mission to manage, develop, and protect water and related resources in an environmentally and economically sound manner in the interest of the American public.

References Cited

Anderson, D.R., Burnham, K.P., and White, G.C., 1994, AIC model selection in overdispersed capture-recapture data: Ecology, v. 75, p. 1780–1793.

Anthony, R.G., Forsman, E.D., Franklin, A.B., Anderson, D.R., Burnham, K.P., White, G.C., Schwarz, C.J., Nichols, J.D., Hines, J.E., Olson, G.S., Ackers, S.H., Andrews, L.S., Biswell, B.L., Carlson, P.C., Diller, L.V., Dugger, K.M., Fehring, K.E., Fleming, T.L., Gerhardt, R.P., Gremel, S.A., Gutiérrez, R.J., Happe, P.J., Herter, D.R., Higley, J.M., Horn, R.B., Irwin, L.L., Loschl, P.J., Reid, J.A., and Sovern, S.G., 2006, Status and trends in demography of northern spotted owls, 1985–2003: Wildlife Monographs, v. 163, 48 p.

Banish, N.P., Adams, B.J., Shively, R.S., Mazur, M.M., Beauchamp, D.A., and Wood, T.M., 2009, Distribution and habitat associations of radio-tagged adult Lost River suckers and shortnose suckers in Upper Klamath Lake, Oregon: Transactions of the American Fisheries Society, v. 138, p. 153–168.

Bradbury, J.P., Colman, S.M., and Reynolds, R.L., 2004, The history of recent limnological changes and human impact on Upper Klamath Lake, Oregon: Journal of Paleolimnology, v. 31, p. 151–165.

Buckland, S.T., Burnham, K.P., and Augustin, N.H., 1997, Model selection: an integral part of inference: Biometrics, v. 53, p. 603–618.

Burnham, K.P., and Anderson, D.R., 2002, Model selection and multimodel inference–A practical information-theoretic approach, 2nd ed.: Springer, New York, 488 p.

Choquet, R., Lebreton, J.D., Gimenez, O., Reboulet, A.M., and Pradel, R., 2009, U-CARE: utilities for performing goodness of fit tests and manipulating CApture-REcapture data: Ecography, v. 32, p. 1071–1074.

Cooch, E., and White, G., 2010, Program MARK–A gentle introduction, 9th ed.: accessed May 16, 2011, at *http://www.phidot.org/software/mark/docs/book/*.

Cooperman, M., and Markle, D.F., 2003, Rapid out-migration of Lost River and shortnose sucker larvae from in-river spawning beds to in-lake rearing grounds: Transactions of the American Fisheries Society, v. 132, p. 1138–1153.

Eilers, J.M., Kann, J., Cornett, J., Moser, K., and St. Amand, A., 2004, Paleolimnological evidence of change in a shallow, hypereutrophic lake: Upper Klamath Lake, Oregon, USA: Hydrobiologia, v. 520, p. 7–18.

Franklin, A.B., 2001, Exploring ecological relationships in survival and estimating rates of population change using Program MARK, *in* Field, R., Warren, R.J., Okarma, H., and Sievert, P.R., eds., Proceedings of the Second International Wildlife Management Congress: The Wildlife Society, Bethesda, Maryland, p. 350–356.

Hewitt, D.A., Janney, E.C., Hayes, B.S., and Shively, R.S., 2010, Improving inferences from fisheries capture-recapture studies through remote detection of PIT tags: Fisheries, v. 35, p. 217–231.

Hines, J.E., and Nichols, J.D., 2002, Investigations of potential bias in the estimation of λ using Pradel's (1996) model for capture-recapture data: Journal of Applied Statistics, v. 29, p. 573–587.

Janney, E.C., Barry, P.M., Hayes, B.S., Shively, R.S., and Scott, A., 2006, Demographic analysis of adult Lost River suckers and shortnose suckers in Upper Klamath Lake and its tributaries, Oregon: Report to the Klamath Area Office of the Bureau of Reclamation, U.S. Geological Survey, Klamath Falls Field Station, Oregon, 42 p.

Janney, E.C., Shively, R.S., Hayes, B.S., Barry, P.M., and Perkins, D., 2008, Demographic analysis of Lost River sucker and shortnose sucker populations in Upper Klamath Lake, Oregon: Transactions of the American Fisheries Society, v. 137, p. 1812–1825.

Janney, E.C., Hayes, B.S., Hewitt, D.A., Barry, P.M., Scott, A., Koller, J., Johnson, M., and Blackwood, G., 2009, Demographics and 2008 run timing of adult Lost River (*Deltistes luxatus*) and shortnose (*Chasmistes brevirostris*) suckers in Upper Klamath Lake, Oregon, 2008: U.S. Geological Survey Open-File Report 2009-1183, 32 p. (Also available at *http://pubs.usgs.gov/of/2009/1183/*.)

Kann, J., and Smith, V.H., 1999, Estimating the probability of exceeding elevated pH values critical to fish populations in a hypereutrophic lake: Canadian Journal of Fisheries and Aquatic Sciences, v. 56, p. 2262–2270.

Laake, J., 2010, RMark: R code for MARK analysis, version 1.9.9: accessed May 16, 2011, at *http://www.phidot.org/software/mark/rmark/*.

Laake, J., and Rexstad, E., 2010, RMark–an alternative approach to building linear models in MARK, in Cooch, E., and White, G., eds., Program MARK–A gentle introduction, 9th ed., Appendix C.

Lindenberg, M.K., Hoilman, G., and Wood, T.M., 2009, Water quality conditions in Upper Klamath and Agency Lakes, Oregon, 2006: U.S. Geological Survey Scientific Investigations Report 2008-5201, 54 p. (Also available at *http://pubs.usgs.gov/sir/2008/5201/*.)

Markle, D.F., and Cooperman, M.S., 2002, Relationships between Lost River and shortnose sucker biology and management of Upper Klamath Lake, in Braunworth, W.S., Jr., Welch, T., and Hathaway, R., eds., Water allocation in the Klamath Reclamation Project, 2001: Special Report 1037, Oregon State University Extension Service, Corvallis, p. 93–117.

Moyle, P.B., 2002, Inland fishes of California: University of California Press, Berkeley, 502 p.

National Research Council, 2004, Endangered and threatened fishes in the Klamath River Basin–Causes of decline and strategies for recovery: Washington, D.C., The National Academies Press, 397 p.

Nichols, J.D., 2005, Modern open-population capture-recapture models, in Amstrup, S.C., McDonald, T.L., and Manly, B.F.J., eds., Handbook of capture-recapture analysis: Princeton, New Jersey, Princeton University Press, p. 88–123.

Nichols, J.D., and Hines, J.E., 2002, Approaches for the direct estimation of λ, and demographic contributions to λ, using capture-recapture data: Journal of Applied Statistics, v. 29, p. 539–568.

Otis, D.L., Burnham, K.P., White, G.C., and Anderson, D.R., 1978, Statistical inference from capture data on closed animal populations: Wildlife Monographs, v. 62, 135 p.

Perkins, D.L., Kann, J., and Scoppettone, G.G., 2000, The role of poor water quality and fish kills in the decline of endangered Lost River and shortnose suckers in Upper Klamath Lake: U.S. Geological Survey final report to the Bureau of Reclamation, Contract 4-AA-29-12160, Klamath Falls, Oregon, 39 p.

Pollock, K.H., Yoshizaki, J., Fabrizio, M.C., and Schram, S.T., 2007, Factors affecting survival rates of a recovering lake trout population estimated by mark-recapture in Lake Superior, 1969–1996: Transactions of the American Fisheries Society, v. 136, p. 185–194.

Pradel, R., 1996, Utilization of capture-mark-recapture for the study of recruitment and population growth rate: Biometrics, v. 52, p. 703–709.

R Development Core Team, 2010, R: a language and environment for statistical computing: R Foundation for Statistical Computing, Vienna, Austria: accessed May 16, 2011, at *http://www.R-project.org/*.

Scoppettone, G.G., and Vinyard, G., 1991, Life history and management of four endangered lacustrine suckers, in Minckley, W.L., and Deacon, J.E., eds., Battle against extinction–Native fish management in the American West: Tucson, The University of Arizona Press, p. 359–377.

Terwilliger, M.R., Reece, T., and Markle, D.F., 2010, Historic and recent age structure and growth of endangered Lost River and shortnose suckers in Upper Klamath Lake, Oregon: Environmental Biology of Fishes, v. 89, p. 239–252.

Tobin, J.H., 1994, Construction and performance of a portable resistance board weir for counting migrating adult salmon in rivers: Alaska Fisheries Technical Report Number 22, U.S. Fish and Wildlife Service, Kenai.

U.S. Fish and Wildlife Service, 1993, Lost River (*Deltistes luxatus*) and shortnose (*Chasmistes brevirostris*) sucker recovery plan: Portland, Oregon, 108 p.

White, G.C., and Burnham, K.P., 1999, Program MARK: survival rate estimation from populations of marked animals: Bird Study, v. 46 (Supplement), p. S120–S139.

Williams, B.K., Nichols, J.D., and Conroy, M.J., 2002, Analysis and management of animal populations: New York, Academic Press, 817 p.

Wood, T.M., Hoilman, G.R., and Lindenberg, M.K., 2006, Water-quality conditions in Upper Klamath Lake, Oregon, 2002–04: U.S. Geological Survey Scientific Investigations Report 2006-5209, 52 p. (Also available at *http://pubs.usgs.gov/sir/2006/5209/*.)

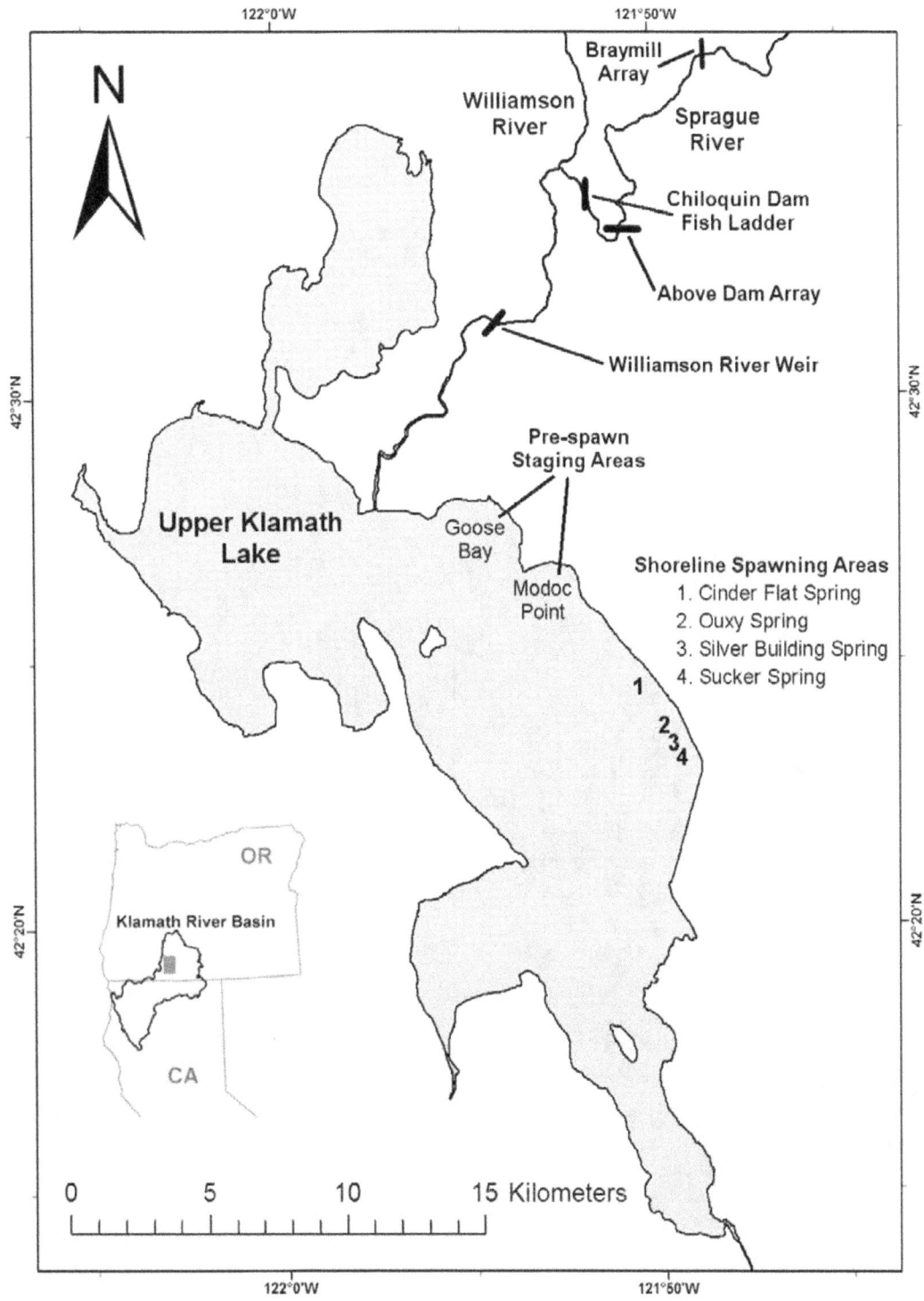

Figure 1. Map showing sampling locations for Lost River suckers and shortnose suckers in Upper Klamath Lake and its tributaries. The inset shows the Klamath River Basin and the location of Upper Klamath Lake in southcentral Oregon.

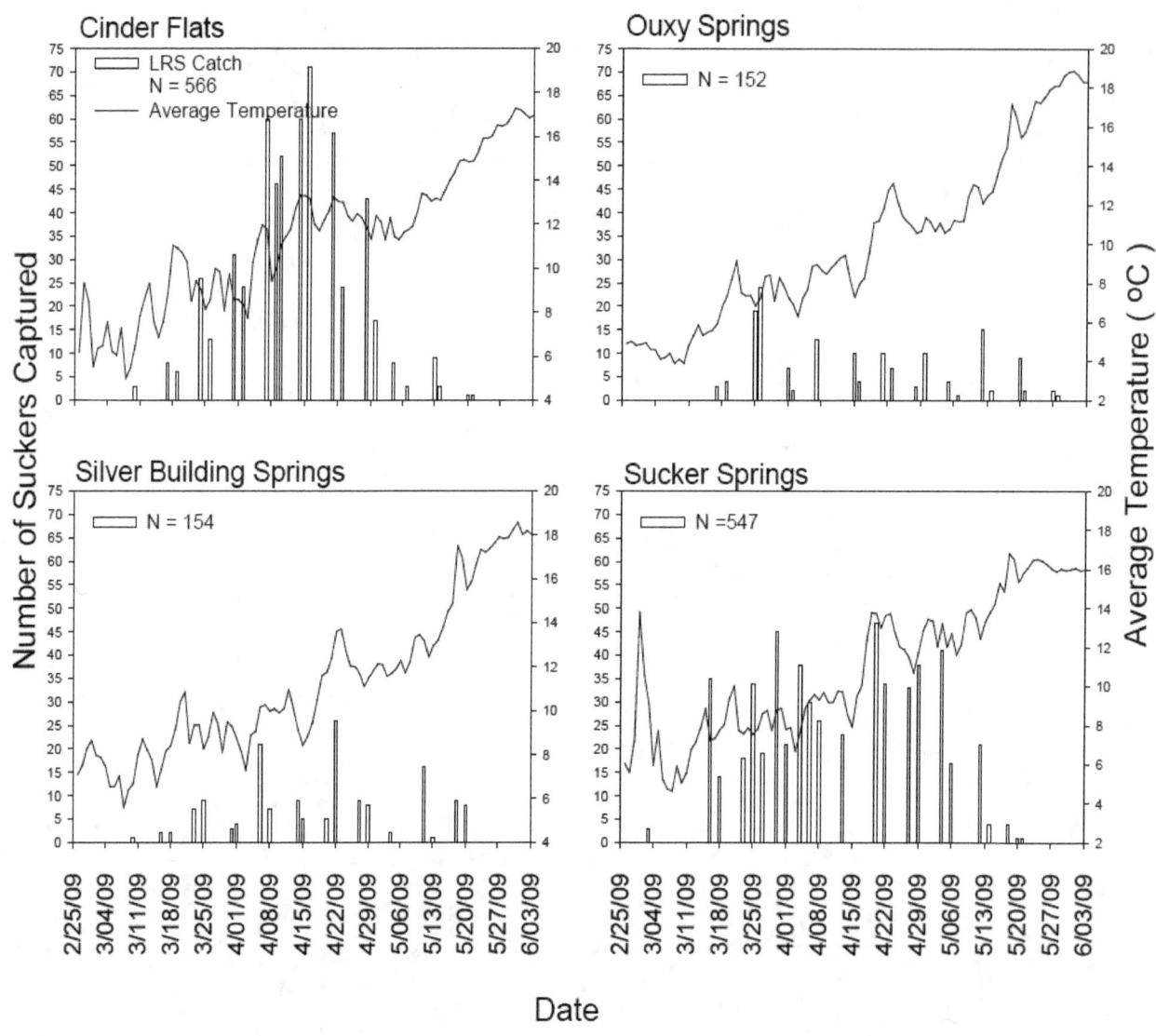

Figure 2. Seasonality of trammel net captures of Lost River suckers at lakeshore springs in Upper Klamath Lake, Oregon, 2009. Average daily water temperature (°C) is reported from temperature loggers that were placed away from spring influence near each sampling location. Only the first capture of an individual at any of the locations is included.

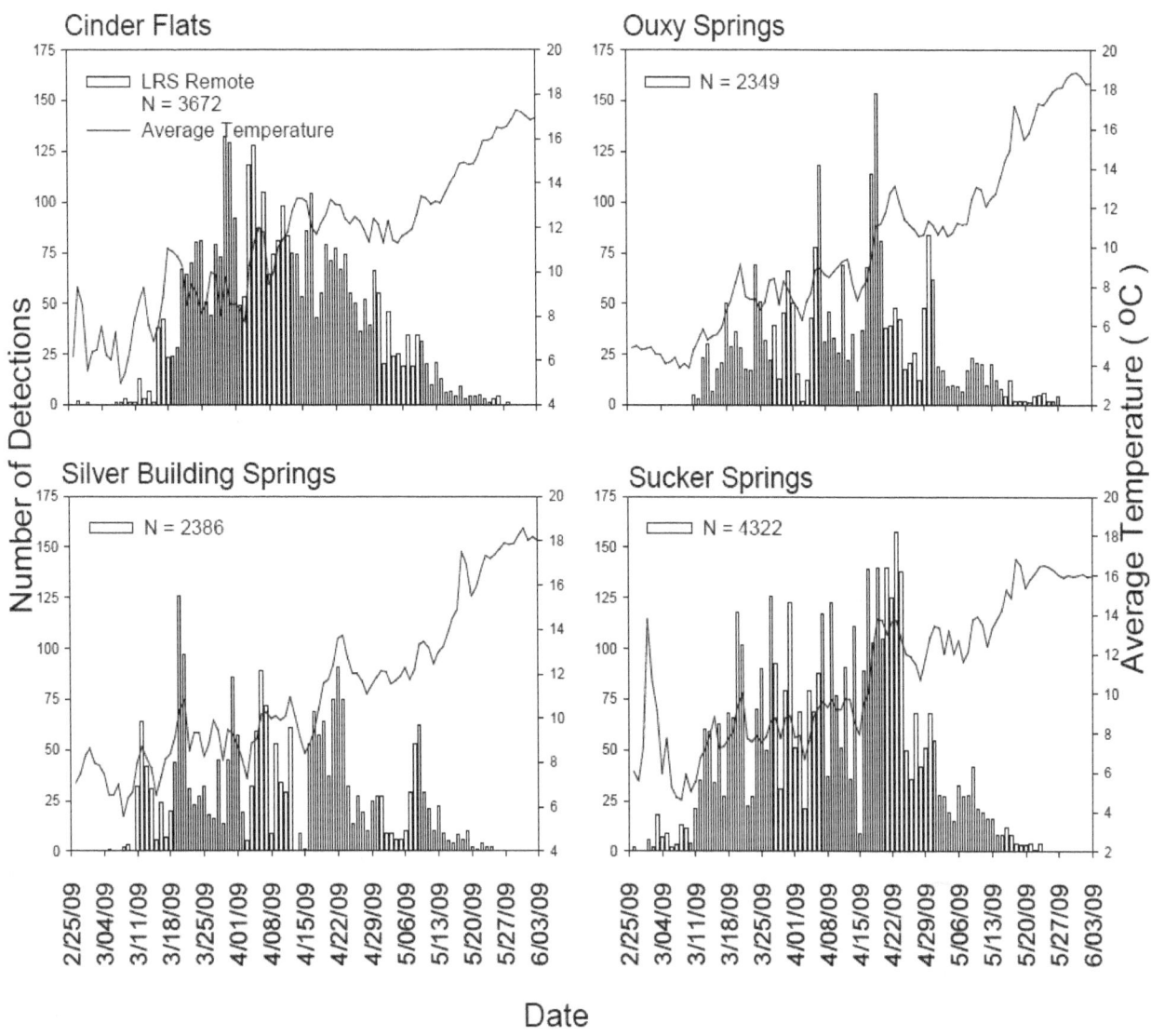

Figure 3. Seasonality of detections of Lost River suckers on remote passive integrated transponder (PIT) tag antennas at lakeshore springs in Upper Klamath Lake, Oregon, 2009. Average daily water temperature (°C) is reported from temperature loggers that were placed away from spring influence near each sampling location. Only the first detection of an individual at a given spring is included, but individuals visited multiple springs during the season.

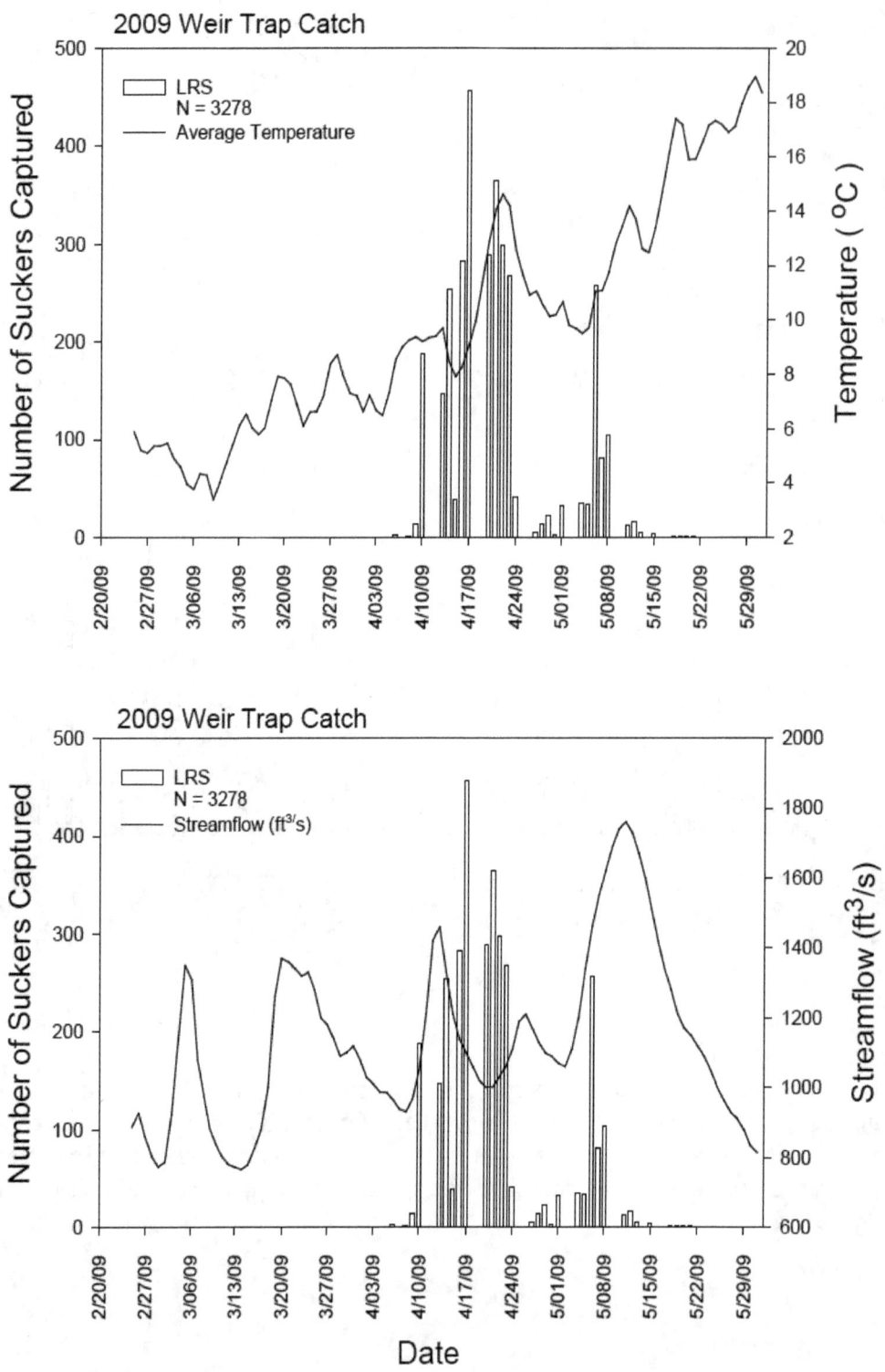

Figure 4. Seasonality of captures of Lost River suckers in the upstream trap of the Williamson River weir during 2009.

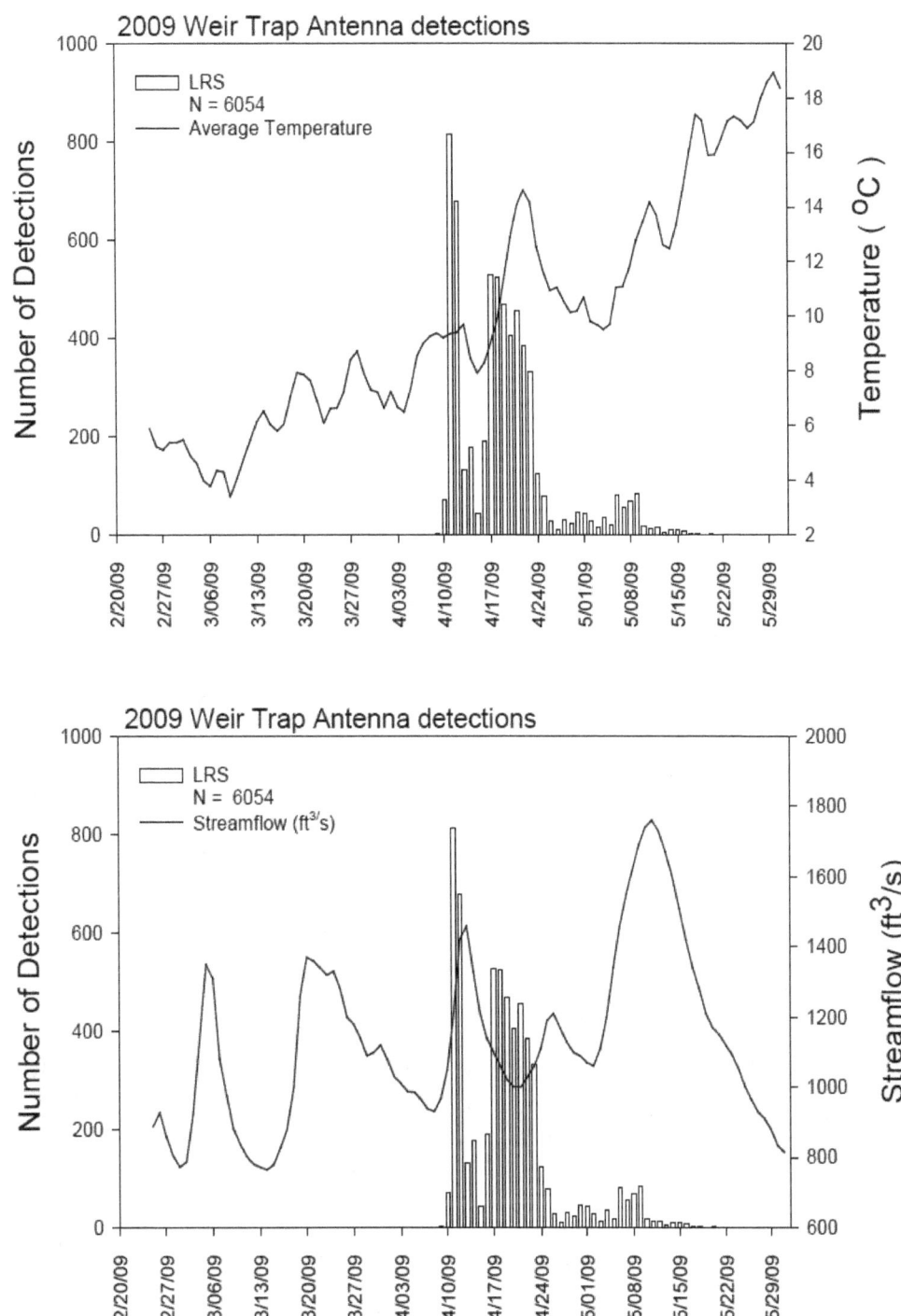

Figure 5. Seasonality of detections of Lost River suckers on the remote passive integrated transponder (PIT) tag antenna at the upstream trap of the Williamson River weir in 2009. Only the first detection of an individual is included.

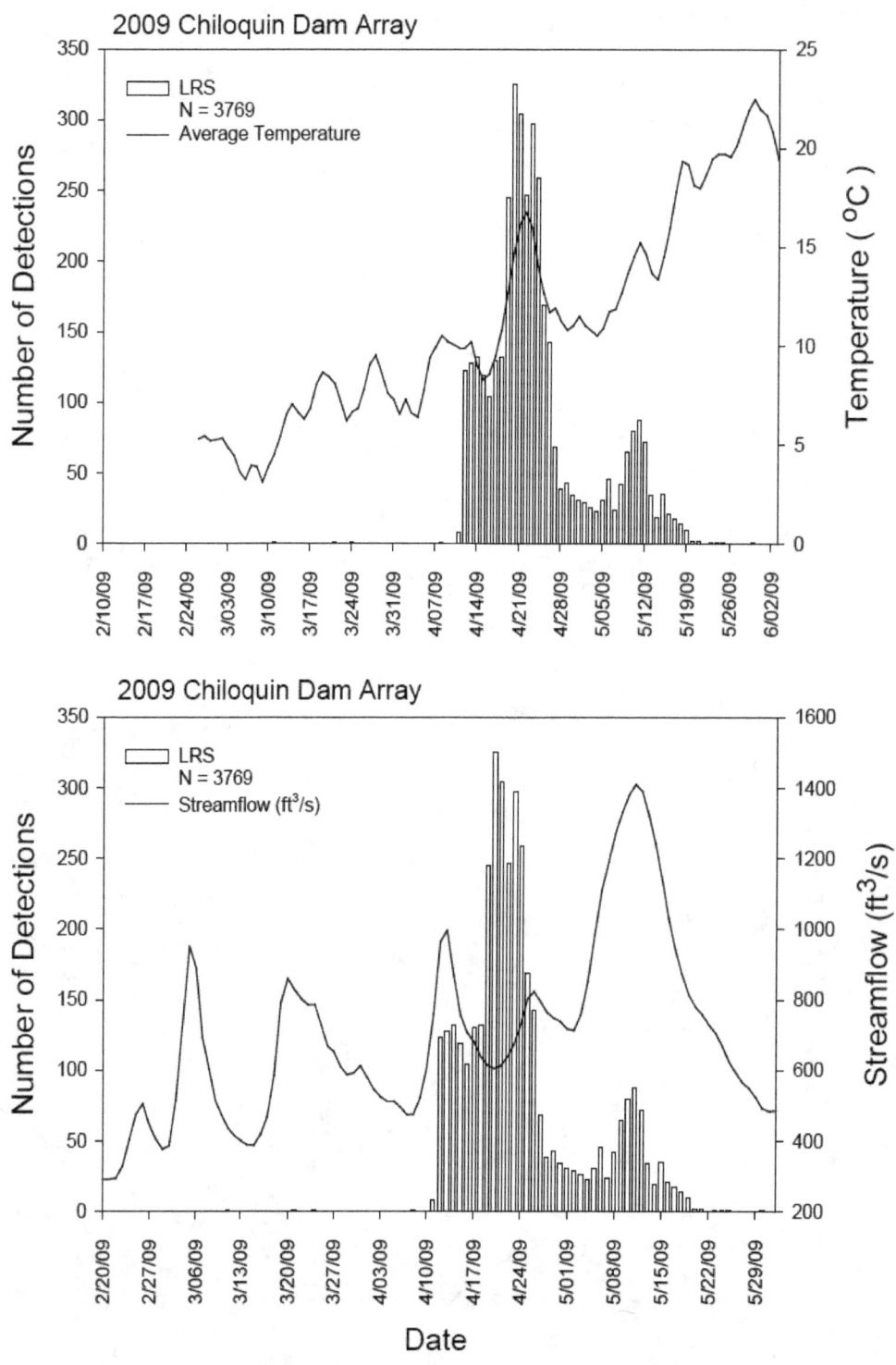

Figure 6. Seasonality of detections of Lost River suckers on the remote passive integrated transponder (PIT) tag antenna array across the Sprague River just downstream of the Chiloquin Dam site in 2009. Only the first detection of an individual is included.

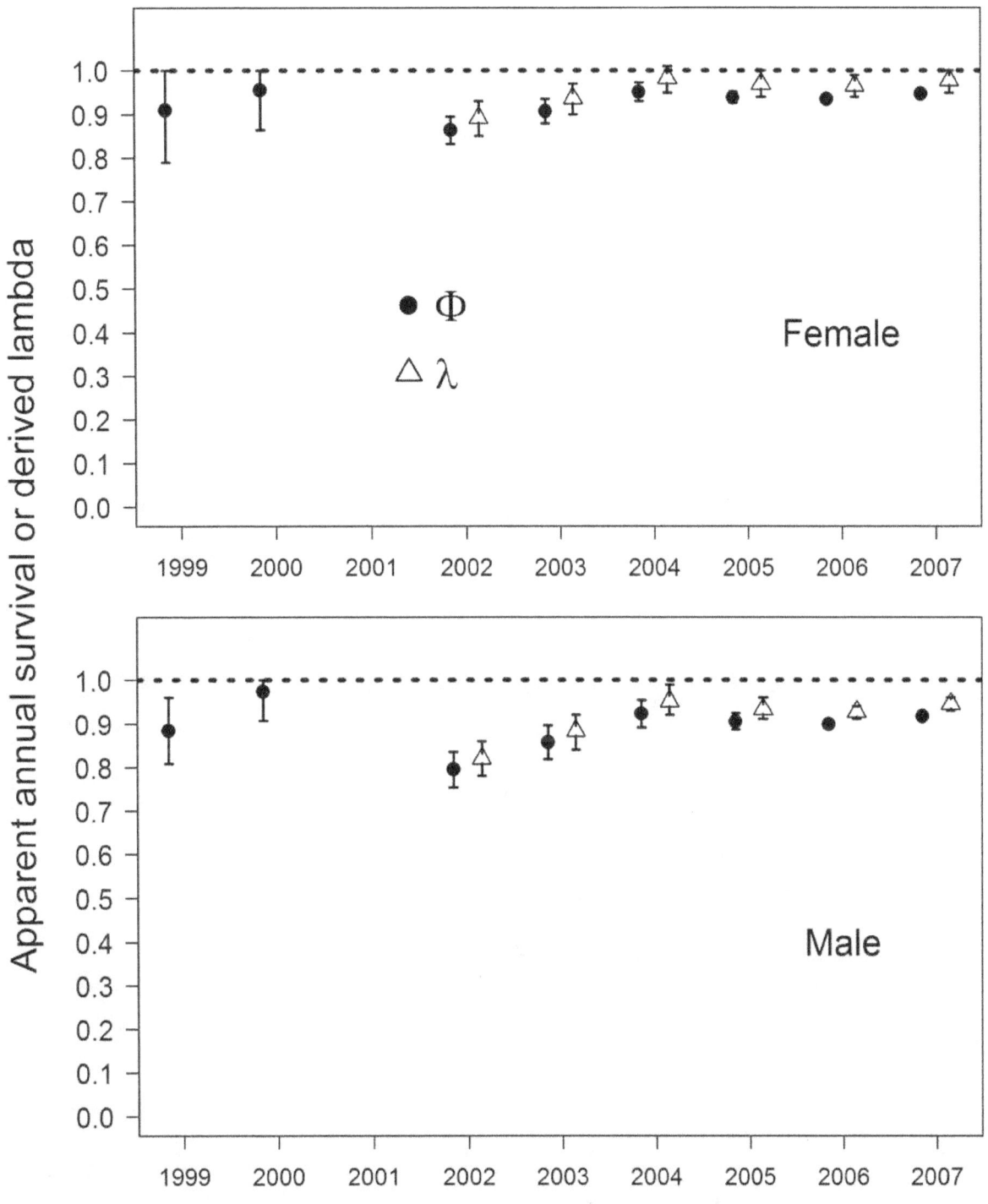

Figure 7. Model-averaged estimates of apparent annual survival probability (Φ) and derived population rate of change (λ) with 95% confidence intervals for Lost River suckers from the lakeshore spawning subpopulation, 1999–2007. The 2001 estimates of Φ were on the boundary at 1.0 and are not shown, as they indicate estimability problems.

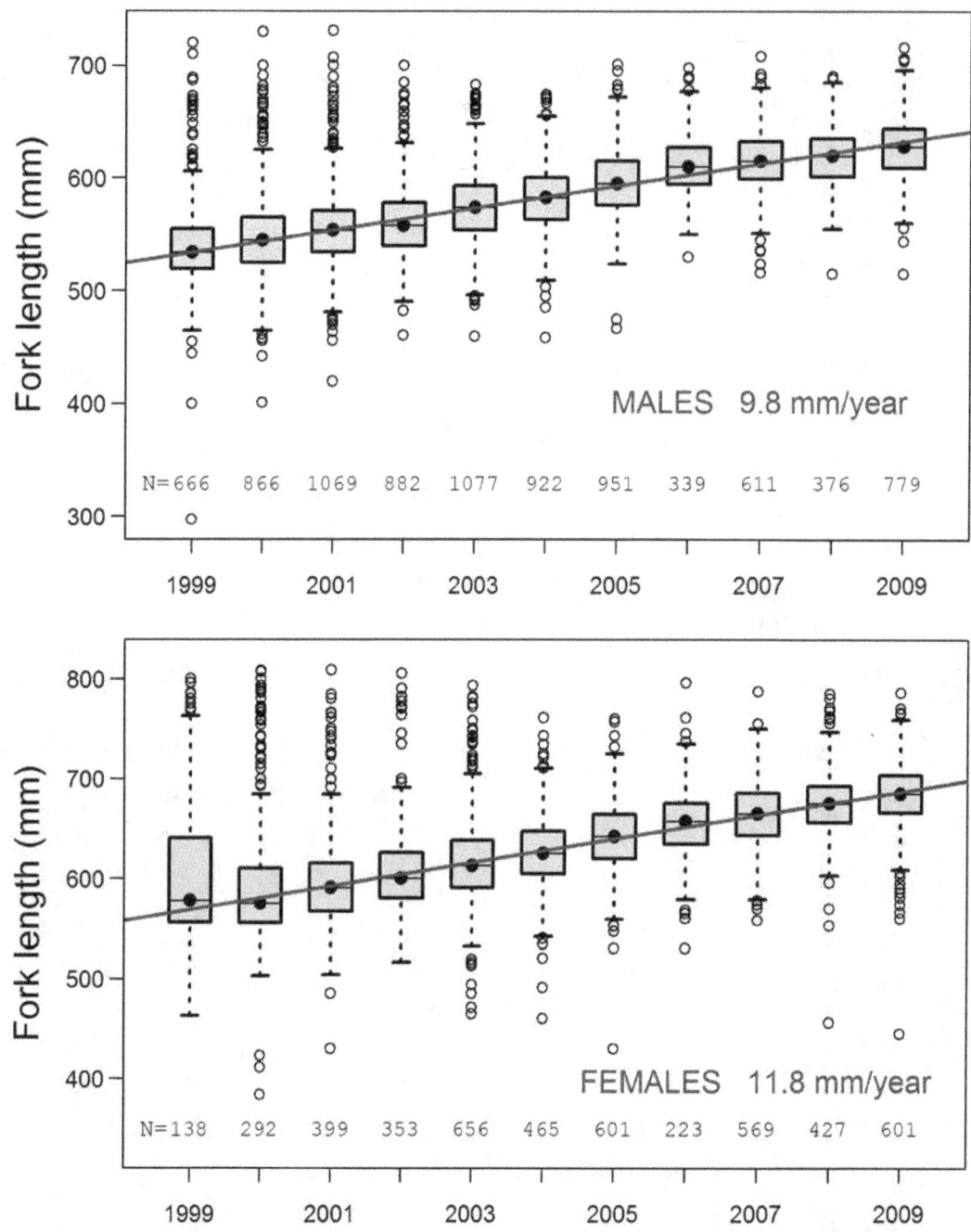

Figure 8. Boxplots of fork lengths of male (*top*) and female (*bottom*) Lost River suckers captured in trammel nets at lakeshore springs, 1999–2009. Dots in the boxes represent the medians and the boxes cover the central 75 percent of the data. The number of fish included in the boxplots for each year are given near the x-axis in each panel. The blue lines are simple linear regressions through the medians and the slope of the regression for each sex is reported as an average annual growth rate.

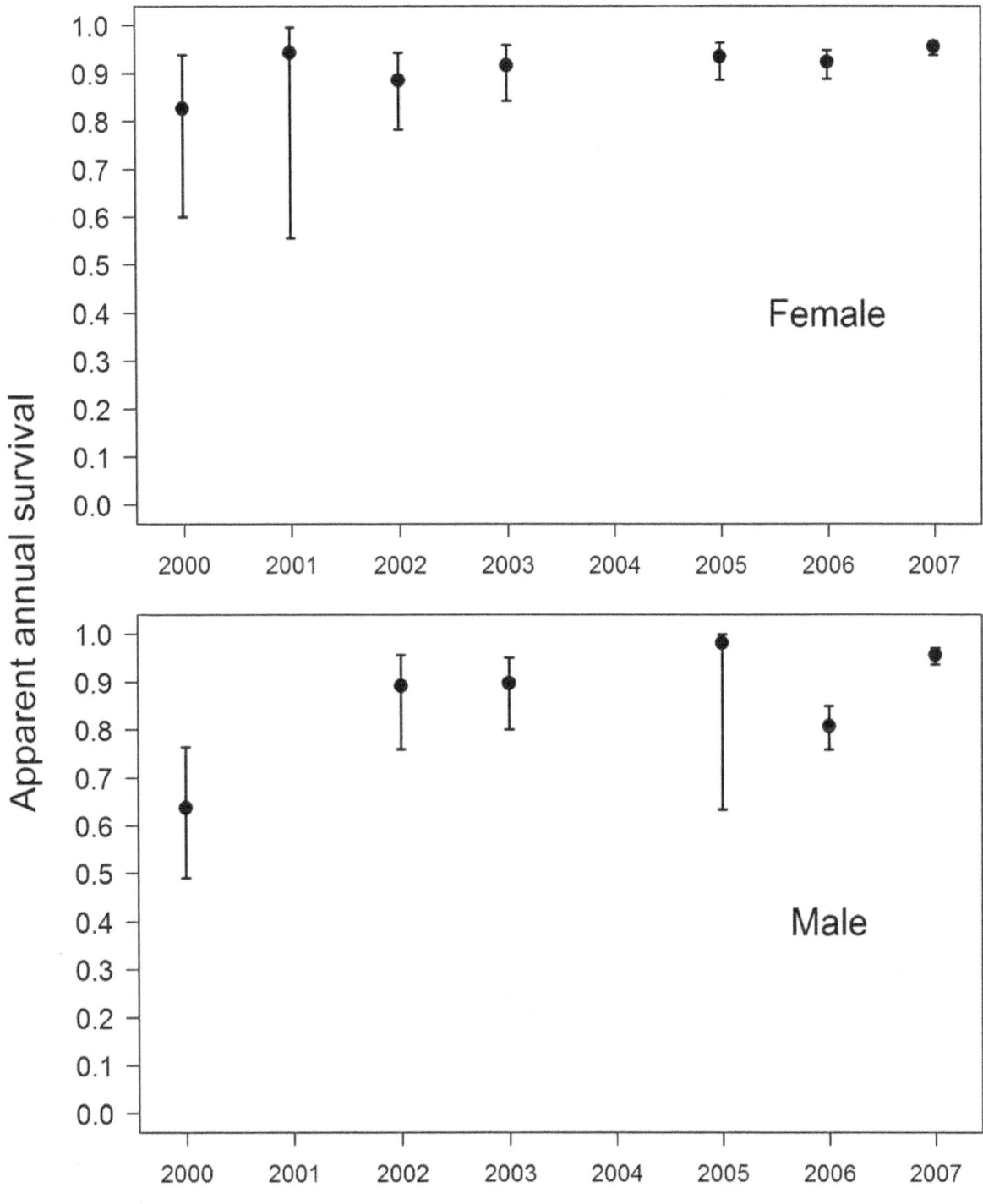

Figure 9. Model-averaged estimates of apparent annual survival probability (Φ) with 95% confidence intervals for Lost River suckers from the river spawning subpopulation, 2000–2007. The estimates for males in 2001 and both sexes in 2004 were on the boundary at 1.0 and are not shown, as they indicate estimability problems.

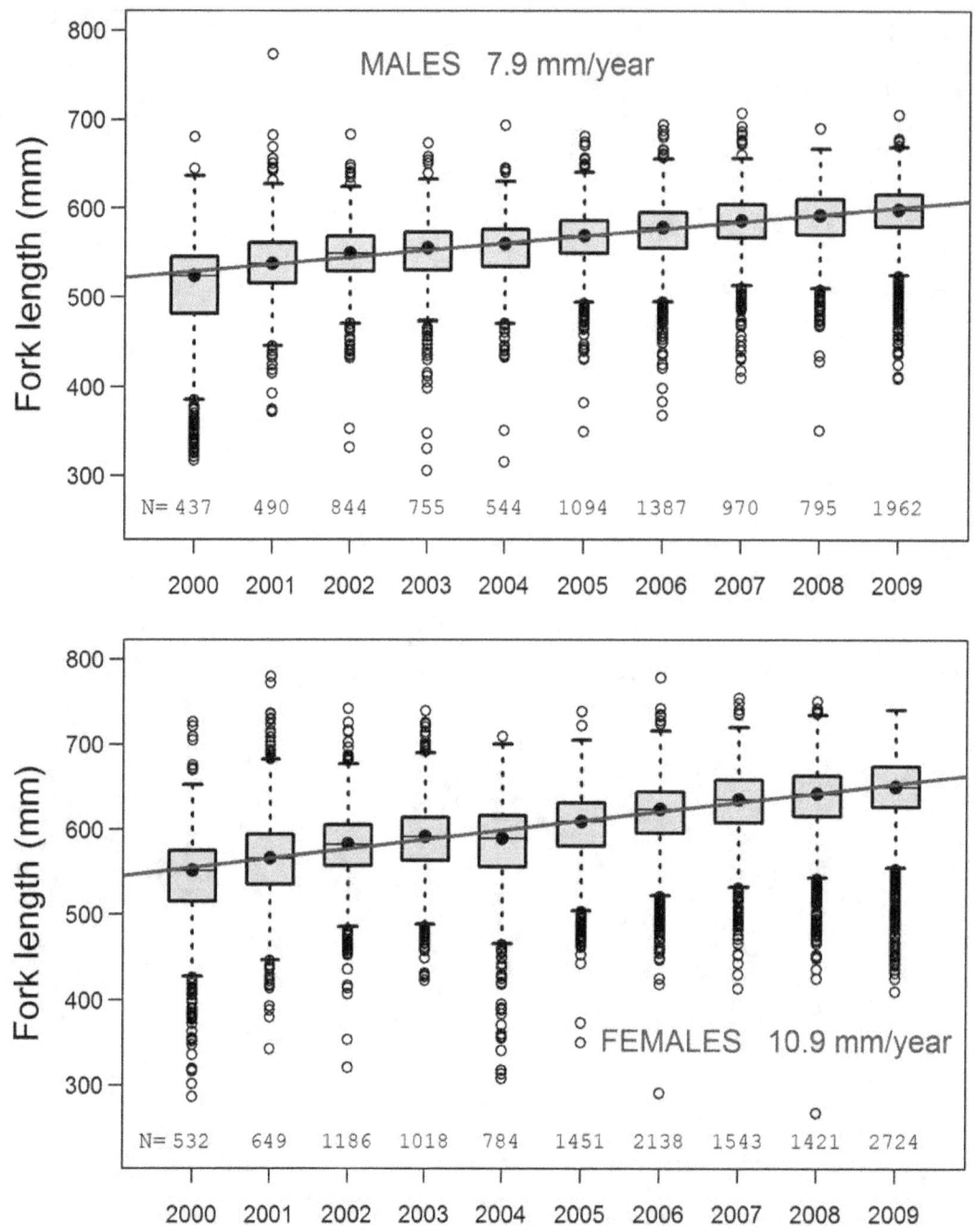

Figure 10. Boxplots of fork lengths of male (*top*) and female (*bottom*) Lost River suckers captured at pre-spawn staging areas in Upper Klamath Lake and in the Williamson and Sprague Rivers, 2000–2009. Dots in the boxes represent the medians and the boxes cover the central 75 percent of the data. The number of fish included in the boxplots for each year are given near the x-axis in each panel. The blue lines are simple linear regressions through the medians and the slope of the regression for each sex is reported as an average annual growth rate.

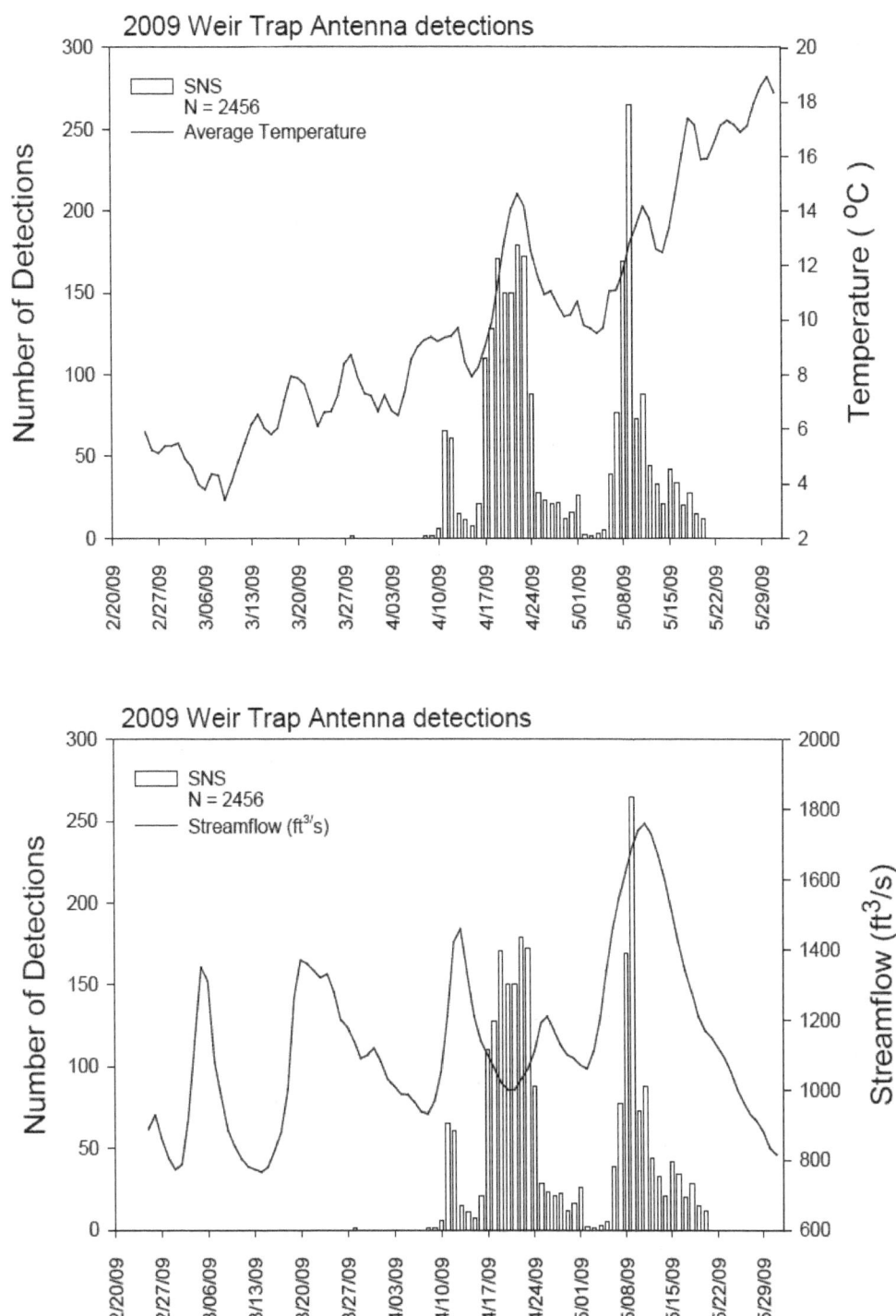

Figure 11. Seasonality of detections of shortnose suckers on the remote passive integrated transponder (PIT) tag antenna at the upstream trap of the Williamson River weir in 2009. Only the first detection of an individual is included.

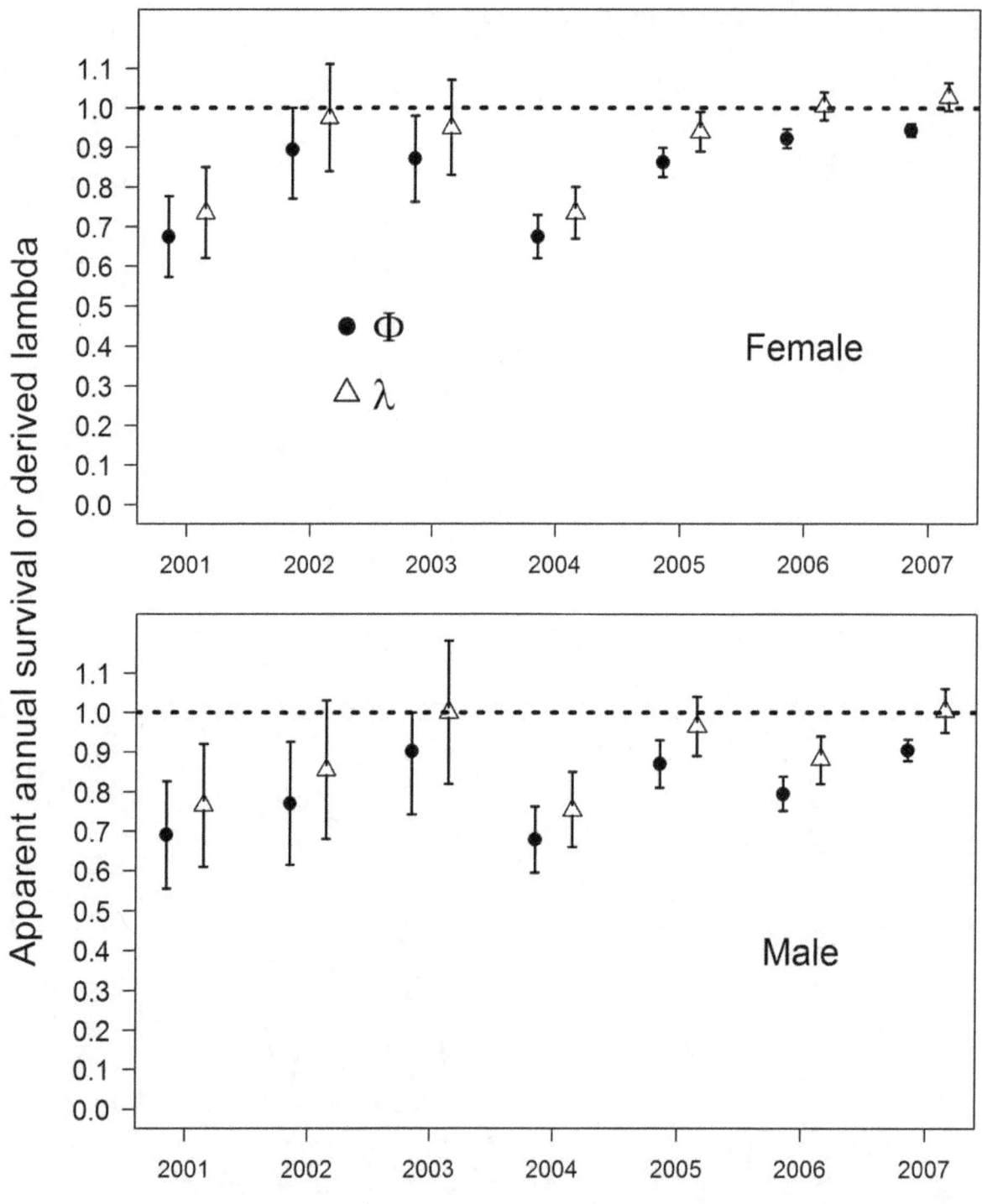

Figure 12. Model-averaged estimates of apparent annual survival probability (Φ) and derived population rate of change (λ) with 95% confidence intervals for shortnose suckers, 2001–2007. The estimates of Φ in 1999 and 2000 were either on the boundary at 1.0 or were so imprecise that they were not useful, so they are not shown.

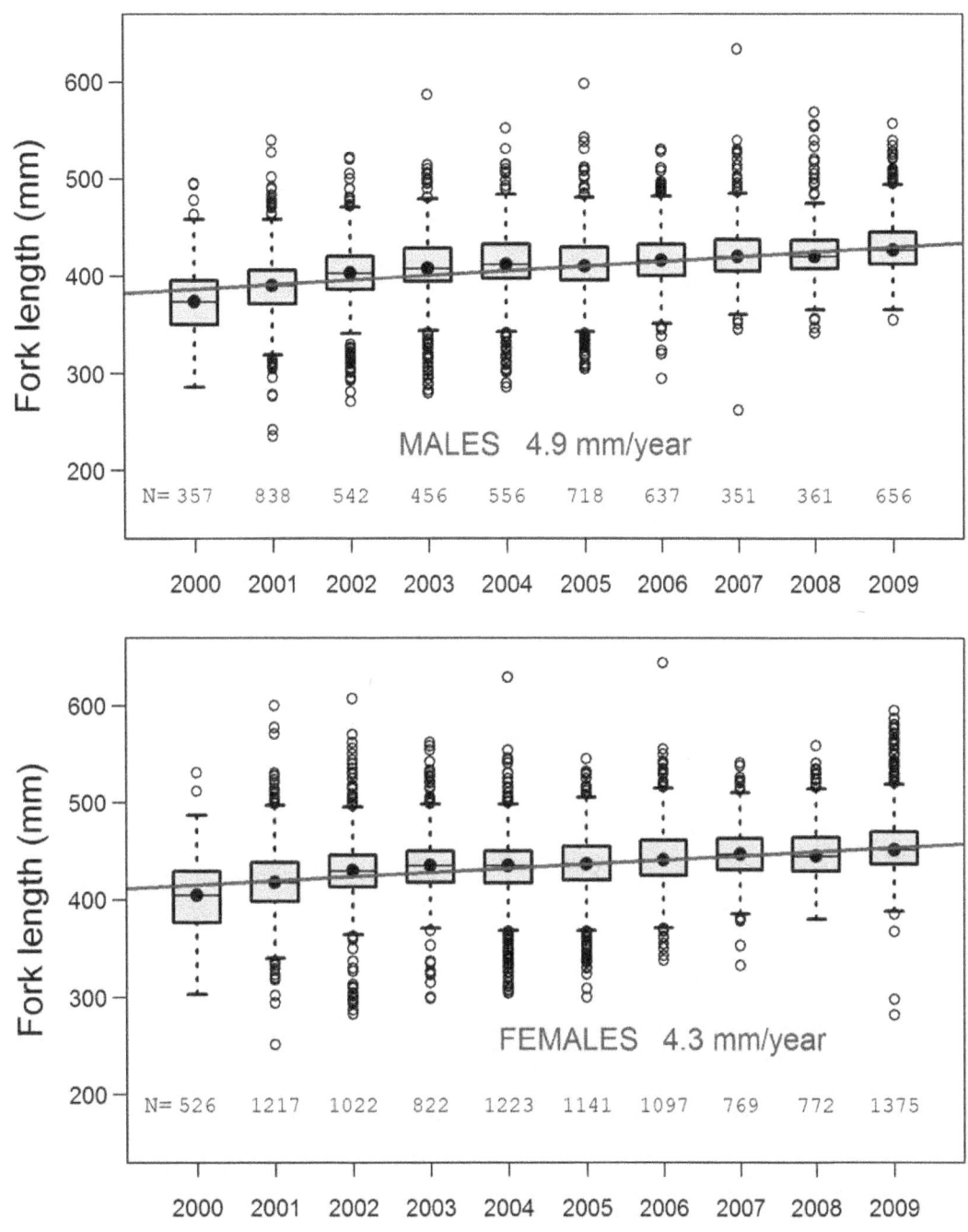

Figure 13. Boxplots of fork lengths of male (*top*) and female (*bottom*) shortnose suckers captured in Upper Klamath Lake and the Williamson and Sprague Rivers, 2000–2009. Dots in the boxes represent the medians and the boxes cover the central 75 percent of the data. The number of fish included in the boxplots for each year are given near the x-axis in each panel. The blue lines are simple linear regressions through the medians and the slope of the regression for each sex is reported as an average annual growth rate.

Table 1. Numbers of Lost River and shortnose suckers captured in Upper Klamath Lake (UKL) and the Williamson River in 2009.

[Totals only include the first capture of an individual at a given location, but individuals may have been captured at more than one location. Recaptures are the percentage of individuals captured in 2009 that were given a passive integrated transponder (PIT) tag in a previous year]

Capture location	Lost River suckers	Recaptures	Shortnose suckers	Recaptures
UKL Pre-spawn Staging Areas	1,569	13%	1,794	25%
Williamson River Weir	3,279	8%	368	25%
UKL Lakeshore Springs	1,419	45%	10	60%

Table 2. Numbers of Lost River and shortnose suckers detected by remote antennas in Upper Klamath Lake (UKL) and its tributaries in 2009.

[Totals only include the first detection of an individual at a given location, but individuals may have been detected at more than one location]

Location of remote antenna(s)	Lost River suckers	Shortnose suckers	Total
Williamson and Sprague Rivers			
Williamson River Weir	12,509	5,023	17,532
Chiloquin Dam Array	3,769	827	4,596
Above Dam Array	901	447	1,348
Braymill Array	83	18	101
UKL Lakeshore Springs			
Cinder Flats	3,672	15	3,687
Ouxy Springs	2,349	12	2,361
Silver Building Springs	2,386	15	2,401
Sucker Springs	4,323	35	4,358

Table 3. Model selection results for the top 10 capture-recapture models fitted to the data for the lakeshore spawning subpopulation of Lost River suckers, 1999–2009.

[Akaike's Information Criterion corrected for small sample size and overdispersion (quasilikelihood AICc [QAICc]) was used to compare the candidate models of survival (Φ) and re-encounter (p) probabilities (overdispersion correction factor [$\hat{c}$] = 1.57). Twenty-five other models were considered, but all had ΔQAICc > 35 and are not shown. In the model names, a × symbol indicates fully interactive effects and the + symbol indicates additive effects. The *tagtype* effect on p in the model name refers to the difference between 125 kHz and 134.2 kHz PIT tags, which is only included for 2006 through 2009. The *tagtype* effect is either constrained to be the same across years (*tagtype* alone) or allowed to vary by year (*tagtype×time*). Both structures were combined additively (+ precedes *tagtype*) and interactively (× precedes *tagtype*) with the other effects in the models. The best model is presented first, and ΔQAICc values represent the difference between the QAICc value of a given model and that of the best model. Akaike weights (w_i) provide a measure of each model's relative weight or likelihood of being the best model in the set given the data. Number of parameters (K) is the total number that is theoretically estimable in the model]

Model	K	QAICc	ΔQAICc	w_i	$-2log_eL$
$\Phi(sex + time)p(sex \times time + [tagtype \times time])$	34	24,857.1	0.00	0.37	38,869.2
$\Phi(sex \times time)p(sex \times time + [tagtype \times time])$	42	24,857.2	0.08	0.35	38,844.1
$\Phi(sex + time)p(sex \times time + tagtype)$	31	24,859.2	2.07	0.13	38,881.8
$\Phi(sex \times time)p(sex \times time + tagtype)$	39	24,859.2	2.11	0.13	38,856.7
$\Phi(sex + time)p(sex \times time \times tagtype)$	38	24,863.7	6.66	0.01	38,867.0
$\Phi(sex \times time)p(sex \times time \times tagtype)$	46	24,863.9	6.76	0.01	38,842.0
$\Phi(sex \times time)p(sex + time + [tagtype \times time])$	33	24,869.8	12.68	0.00	38,892.2
$\Phi(sex + time)p(sex + time + [tagtype \times time])$	25	24,870.3	13.16	0.00	38,918.1
$\Phi(sex + time)p(sex + time + tagtype)$	22	24,872.5	15.41	0.00	38,931.0
$\Phi(sex \times time)p(sex + time + tagtype)$	31	24,874.0	16.90	0.00	38,905.1

Table 4. Model selection results for the top nine capture-recapture models fitted to the data for the river spawning subpopulation of Lost River suckers, 2000–2009.

[Akaike's Information Criterion corrected for small sample size and overdispersion (quasilikelihood AICc [QAICc]) was used to compare the candidate models of survival (Φ) and re-encounter (p) probabilities (overdispersion correction factor [$\hat{c}$] = 3.23). Twenty-six other models were considered, but all had ΔQAICc > 50 and are not shown. See the caption note for table 3 for a complete description of table contents]

Model	K	QAICc	ΔQAICc	w_i	$-2log_eL$
$\Phi(sex \times time)p(sex \times time \times tagtype)$	42	15,920.1	0.00	0.91	51,150.3
$\Phi(sex + time)p(sex \times time \times tagtype)$	35	15,925.2	5.04	0.07	51,211.9
$\Phi(sex \times time)p(sex \times time + [tagtype \times time])$	38	15,928.0	7.91	0.02	51,201.8
$\Phi(sex + time)p(sex \times time + [tagtype \times time])$	31	15,936.9	16.75	0.00	51,275.7
$\Phi(time)p(sex \times time \times tagtype)$	34	15,938.1	17.93	0.00	51,260.0
$\Phi(sex + time)p(sex + time + [tagtype \times time])$	23	15,950.1	29.99	0.00	51,370.2
$\Phi(time)p(sex \times time + [tagtype \times time])$	30	15,957.3	37.14	0.00	51,348.0
$\Phi(sex \times time)p(sex + time + [tagtype \times time])$	30	15,964.3	44.12	0.00	51,370.5
$\Phi(time)p(sex + time + [tagtype \times time])$	22	15,969.4	49.27	0.00	51,438.9

Table 5. Model selection results for the top six capture-recapture models fitted to the data for the shortnose sucker population, 1999–2009.

[Akaike's Information Criterion corrected for small sample size and overdispersion (quasilikelihood AICc [QAICc]) was used to compare the candidate models of survival (Φ) and re-encounter (p) probabilities (overdispersion correction factor [$\hat{c}$] = 2.09). Twenty-nine other models were considered, but all had ΔQAICc > 30 and are not shown. See the caption note for table 3 for a complete description of table contents]

Model	K	QAICc	ΔQAICc	w_i	$-2log_eL$
$\Phi(sex \times time)p(sex + time + [tagtype \times time])$	33	19,504.7	0.00	1.00	40,626.7
$\Phi(sex \times time)p(sex \times time + [tagtype \times time])$	42	19,516.4	11.73	0.00	40,613.5
$\Phi(sex \times time)p(sex \times time \times tagtype)$	46	19,519.8	15.12	0.00	40,603.8
$\Phi(sex + time)p(sex + time + [tagtype \times time])$	25	19,521.6	16.88	0.00	40,695.5
$\Phi(sex + time)p(sex \times time + [tagtype \times time])$	34	19,525.5	20.79	0.00	40,666.0
$\Phi(sex + time)p(sex \times time \times tagtype)$	38	19,529.4	24.69	0.00	40,657.3

www.ingramcontent.com/pod-product-compliance
Lightning Source LLC
Chambersburg PA
CBHW080347290526
45791CB00009BA/2765